Mary and Ed

Christmas 1976

Floyd & Marty

An Enduring Heritage

Woodside Store

An Enduring Heritage

Historic Buildings of the San Francisco Peninsula

DOROTHY F. REGNERY

Dorothy F. Regnery

Photographs by Jack E. Boucher

Sponsored by the Junior League of Palo Alto, Inc.

in cooperation with the Historic American Buildings Survey

of the National Park Service

Stanford University Press, Stanford, California   1976

Stanford University Press
Stanford, California
© 1976 by the Board of Trustees of the
Leland Stanford Junior University
Printed in the United States of America
ISBN 0-8047-0918-1
LC 76-14272

Foreword

Now the oldest nationwide federal program in historic preservation, the Historic American Buildings Survey (HABS) is our national record of the building arts in the United States. Based on a proposal by Charles E. Peterson in November 1933 in response to the passage of the act establishing the Civil Works Administration, the Survey was initiated both to document our rapidly disappearing architectural heritage and to provide temporary economic relief for architects during the Depression. Organizationally, the program was—and remains—a collaborative effort of the National Park Service, the American Institute of Architects, and the Library of Congress.

In the first phase of HABS recording, the country was divided into 39 districts, each with a District Officer nominated by the local chapters of the American Institute of Architects and appointed by the Secretary of the Interior. California was initially divided into two districts: Northern California, that part of the state "north of San Luis Obispo and the Tehachapi"; and Southern California, which also included Arizona. Within a year, increased recording activity necessitated the division of the state into four districts. In both divisions, San Mateo County was located in the Northern District, headquartered in San Francisco. In spite of the extensive recording undertaken in the state, however, only one San Mateo County building— the Francisco Sanchez House (CAL-156) in the San Pedro Valley—was recorded during the first

decade of HABS. During these early years, first consideration generally was given to the earliest buildings in each state. In California, the missions and related structures received the most extensive coverage.

With the advent of World War II, federal employment projects initiated during the Depression came to a halt. From 1941 to 1956 the HABS collections continued to grow through donations, principally from the National Park Service. In the 1950's, when the program was reactivated, the country was in the midst of a building boom and few architects were available to produce the detailed architectural drawings that are the basis of the Survey's archival collections. HABS found that architectural students, free during the summer recess, were a pool of eager and talented draftsmen. Summer field teams of four or five architectural students and a project historian under the supervision of a professor of architecture are now the primary source for new documentary records. In addition to producing quality records for the Survey, these summer projects afford many future architects their first experience in architectural history and historic preservation.

Although the present HABS program is considerably smaller than in the 1930's, the Survey has one of the largest national collections of its kind in the world. It includes 35,000 sheets of measured drawings, 45,000 photographs, and 16,000 pages of written historical and architectural data for over 17,000 structures in the United States, Puerto Rico, and the Virgin Islands. In California, the Survey has records for approximately 1,100 structures. Copies of the original California records at the Library of Congress are housed at the California Historical Society in San Francisco. Public accessibility has always been an important aspect of the HABS archives; therefore, to assist users of the collection, catalogs listing the Survey's holdings are published periodically. Copies of all HABS records may be ordered from the Library of Congress. A catalog for the State of California has been prepared as a cooperative project with the California Historical Society for publication in 1977.

Contributions—whether in services or in funds —from individuals, private organizations, and public agencies have been essential for the Survey's continuing existence. In 1974 the Junior League of Palo Alto joined forces with a Survey team to record examples of historic architecture in San Mateo County. The team, headquartered at the League's offices in Menlo Park, was composed of Professor Kim Spurgeon, Project Supervisor (Kansas State University); Patrick Christopher, Historian (Columbia University); Stephen Farneth, Student Architect (Carnegie-Mellon University); Robert Randall, Student Architect (University of Houston); Amy Weinstein, Student Architect (University of Pennsylvania); and Aino Viera da Rosa, Student Assistant Architect (University of Oregon). The architectural measured drawings and written historical data produced in 1974—and the photographs taken by the HABS staff photographer, Jack Boucher, in 1975 —form the basis for this publication.

In February 1973 I had the opportunity to meet Dorothy Farris Regnery, whose concern for the historic and architectural heritage of San Mateo County resulted in conversations that eventually brought the HABS to Menlo Park. Also from inception to completion, the support of Kathryn H. Kaiser, Chairman of the Junior League's Community Heritage Project, assured our success. The summer program in 1974 and *An Enduring Heritage* would have been impossible without the devoted and sustained efforts of these two exceptional persons. We wish to thank them and the Community Heritage Committee for their help, and to applaud their determined efforts to protect the man-made environment on the Peninsula.

John Poppeliers
Chief, Historic American
Buildings Survey

Preface

IN THE FALL of 1972, members of the Junior League of Palo Alto met to discuss ways of alerting the surrounding area to its architectural heritage. Out of this meeting grew the Community Heritage Project and this book, a record of the Peninsula's history as seen through its most significant extant buildings.

In addition to League members, community volunteers were invited to enroll in a year-long training program covering local history, architecture, and methods of research. In 1973 a block-by-block visual survey of San Mateo County was undertaken, yielding candid photographs, addresses, and data on some 1,100 buildings with a claim to historic interest. An evaluation of these buildings by eighteen professional consultants reduced the number to 225 buildings deemed sufficiently interesting to be worthy of research in depth. This figure also reflects a narrowing of the Project's focus to the period 1850-1920, eliminating the three existing pre-1850 structures as over-restored or reconstructed and post-1920 buildings as too difficult to assess historically.

During the period of study and research, the Project's members became aware of the Historic American Buildings Survey (HABS), a division of the National Park Service of the Department of the Interior. In January 1974 the Junior League and the National Park Service reached agreement on a matching grant for an HABS survey of thirteen San Mateo County buildings chosen jointly by the Project and HABS. This professional survey, carried out in the summer of 1974, yielded a series of measured drawings for eight of the buildings, a number of which appear in this volume.

Publication arrangements were then discussed with Stanford University Press, at whose recommendation the number of buildings to be covered in the book was fixed at about fifty and the geographical coverage was expanded to include the northernmost part of Santa Clara County. Dorothy F. Regnery of Portola Valley, an enthusiastic supporter of the Project from its outset, was enlisted by the Junior League to supply historical documentation and photographs, and the League also obtained the services of a professional writer-editor, Margery Wolf. Members of the HABS reviewed the text for its architectural accuracy, and HABS also undertook to supply current photographs of all the structures chosen, a much larger number than in the original contract. The photographs were taken in late summer 1975 by HABS staff photographer Jack E. Boucher.

This volume has two goals. One is to record and document as of 1975 what one Project member has called "the best of the last," the chief remaining elements of the San Francisco Peninsula's architectural heritage. The other is to supply a basis for preserving this heritage so far as may be possible against the ravages of time, neglect, and demolition. One of the buildings chosen for this book, Isaac Graham's White House (pp. 13-14), burned to the ground in February 1976. Others are endangered in different ways, among them the Bank of San Mateo County, the San Mateo County Courthouse, and the Hostess House. As a practical step, the sponsors of this Project plan to apply for the inclusion of all these buildings in the National Register of Historic Places, the nation's official inventory of properties worthy of preservation for their historic value. But no mere listing will be of any help without an active commitment by community officials and residents to the cause of keeping these buildings intact and in good repair.

On behalf of the Community Heritage Project, I would like to acknowledge the fine support we have received from the staffs of the Historic American Buildings Survey and Stanford University Press. In particular, we are grateful to HABS for Jack Boucher's remarkable photographs and the measured drawings prepared by architectural draftsmen employed by the National Park Service, and to Stanford University Press for Albert Burkhardt's handsome design.

Consultants who assisted the Project to its completion were Clyde Arbuckle; Thomas Church; George Courtney, A.I.A.; Herbert J. Dengler; Dr. Elliot Evans; Susan Field; Jean Finch; John L. Frisbee III; Aaron Gallup; Dr. David Gebhard; Virginia Ross Geller; Dr. Walter Horn; Paul C. Johnson; A. Lewis Koué, A.I.A.; Linda Mansfield; John Michael; Michael Painter; Walter Sontheimer, A.I.A.; David Tucker; and John Volpiano. Special thanks are due to Dr. Paul Turner of Stanford University for his assistance in the early stages. We are grateful to Menlo College for graciously hosting five members of the HABS team during their summer stay. We thank the various owners of the properties for their permission to include the structures in the text. Numerous individuals gave our researchers precious hours of their time, notably Birge M. Clark, A.I.A., Dr. Robert Judson Clark, Randall Makinson, Mr. and Mrs. Mortimer Fleishhacker, Dr. James T. Watkins IV, and Jack Walsh and Paul Mobley of the U.S. Coast Guard. To these and innumerable others, the Junior League of Palo Alto wishes to express gratitude.

Kathryn H. Kaiser
Chairman, Community
Heritage Project

Contents

Sources of Illustrations

The 1975 photographs and the measured architectural drawings are from the Historic American Buildings Survey of the National Park Service. The sketches on the frontispiece and pp. 11, 21, 23, and 94 were drawn for this book by Mary Davey. The other photographs and drawings were obtained by the author from the various printed sources, archives, and private collections indicated below. Numbers at the left of each item are pages.

3, 4. *Moore & DePue's Illustrated History of San Mateo County, California* (San Francisco, 1878).

5, 9. Courtesy of Dorothy F. Regnery.

22. *Moore & DePue's Illustrated History of San Mateo County, California* (San Francisco, 1878).

34, 36 (lower left). Courtesy of U.S. Coast Guard.

41. Edward Vischer, *Vischer's Pictorial of California* (San Francisco, 1870). Courtesy of the Bancroft Library, Berkeley, California.

43. Courtesy of the Library of Congress.

46. Courtesy of James T. Watkins IV.

48. Courtesy of City of Menlo Park.

54. Britton & Reyes lithograph. Courtesy of Herbert J. Dengler.

56. Courtesy of San Mateo County Historical Association.

57 (top). Courtesy of the Library of Congress.

58 (lower left), 62 (bottom). Courtesy of Dorothy F. Regnery.

62 (top). Courtesy of Junior League of San Francisco.

67, 70, 71 (lower right), 72 (lower left), 74, 75, 76 (top left), 82 (lower left). Courtesy of Stanford University Archives.

73 (top). Courtesy of Dorothy F. Regnery.

84 (bottom). Courtesy of Dr. and Mrs. Hadley Kirkman, from the original blueprint by A. B. Clark.

86. Courtesy of Birge M. Clark.

87 (top). Courtesy of Facilities Planning Department, Stanford University.

102 (bottom). Courtesy of Dorothy F. Regnery.

112 (top). Courtesy of F. Bourn Hayne.

114 (bottom). Drawing by William Smart, 1976.

115. Courtesy of Palo Alto Historical Association.

117. Courtesy of the Junior League of Palo Alto; photograph by Ron Willis, 1976.

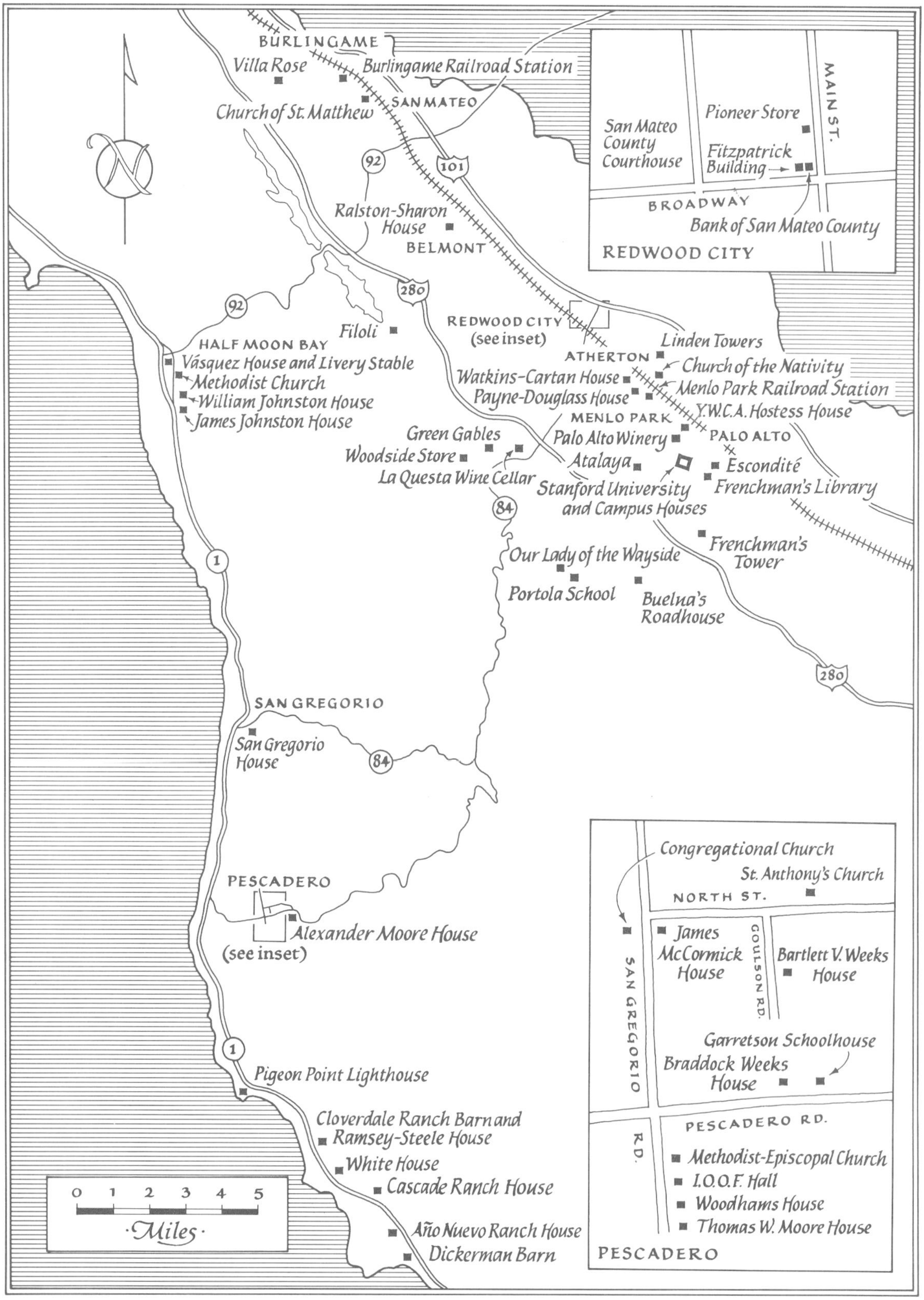
BURLINGAME
Villa Rose
Burlingame Railroad Station
Church of St. Matthew
SAN MATEO
92
101
Ralston-Sharon House
BELMONT
280
92
Filoli
REDWOOD CITY (see inset)
HALF MOON BAY
Vásquez House and Livery Stable
Methodist Church
William Johnston House
James Johnston House
Linden Towers
ATHERTON
Church of the Nativity
Watkins-Cartan House
Menlo Park Railroad Station
Payne-Douglass House
Y.W.C.A. Hostess House
MENLO PARK
Green Gables
Palo Alto Winery
PALO ALTO
Woodside Store
Atalaya
Escondité
La Questa Wine Cellar
Stanford University and Campus Houses
Frenchman's Library
84
Frenchman's Tower
1
Our Lady of the Wayside
Portola School
Buelna's Roadhouse
280
SAN GREGORIO
San Gregorio House
84
PESCADERO
Alexander Moore House
(see inset)
1
Pigeon Point Lighthouse
Cloverdale Ranch Barn and Ramsey-Steele House
White House
Cascade Ranch House
Año Nuevo Ranch House
Dickerman Barn
0 1 2 3 4 5
Miles
MAIN ST.
Pioneer Store
San Mateo County Courthouse
Fitzpatrick Building
BROADWAY
Bank of San Mateo County
REDWOOD CITY
Congregational Church
St. Anthony's Church
NORTH ST.
James McCormick House
GOULSON RD.
Bartlett V. Weeks House
SAN GREGORIO RD.
Garretson Schoolhouse
Braddock Weeks House
PESCADERO RD.
Methodist-Episcopal Church
I.O.O.F. Hall
Woodhams House
Thomas W. Moore House
PESCADERO

Chapter One

Strangers on the Peninsula
1850's-1870's

In the 1830's the Californio population (early settlers holding Mexican citizenship) on the San Francisco Peninsula was probably no more than 150. Modern accounts tend to either romanticize or deplore their relaxed style of life, but even the most critical observer would agree that they were socially and politically ill-equipped to cope with the greedy, enterprising, and often unprincipled strangers about to engulf them. Their economy was based on strong, tough cattle that foraged for themselves. Their debts were recorded in the number of hides owed, and the vast majority of these gentleman landowners on horseback were illiterate. Most Californios on the peninsula received their ranchos after secularization of the missions in 1833, and the surveying of their land was a social event that gave much pleasure to the participants but little proof of their boundaries. Whether the line ran through one hill or the next seemed hardly to matter when the land was so vast and the cattle would graze where they pleased.

A few hunters and trappers began to drift in over the Sierra, but they, like the Yankee traders who carried off the hides and tallow, were dealt with as individuals, and the few who decided to stay were accepted as oddities. An occasional dissatisfied sailor jumped ship and disappeared for a while into the redwoods to set up a still, or to fell trees and split enough shingles to keep him in food and drink. Sometimes the strangers were troublesome neighbors, but in general they were useful. Indeed, in the revolt of 1836 that established California's brief independence from Mexico, Juan Bautista Alvarado and José Castro found them extremely valuable. They were accustomed to living by their wits and their guns, and under the leadership of Isaac Graham they played an important role in the 1836 revolt. But the arrogance some of them showed after this episode was a sad portent of what was to come.

The trickle of strangers passing through the peninsula in the 1830's became a stream in the

Redwood City Embarcadero, 1878

Cascade Ranch House, 1878

1840's. In 1848 in the redwoods near Woodside a little settlement had been established by deserters from the occupying U.S. Army, but it disappeared almost overnight when they heard the news about the glittering pebbles found by John Sutter's carpenter. Other strangers soon took their place. The sleepy provincial town of San Francisco suddenly was required to provide the services of a city, receiving and passing on men and supplies in ever increasing numbers. Merchants were short of everything, from axe handles to beans. There were no buildings to store the goods that arrived or to house the men waiting to move on. There were not enough restaurants to feed them, saloons to entertain them, or banks to hold their gold. There was too little wharf space for the ships filling the bay, and too few warehouses. And hardly had a block of buildings been put up when a fire burnt it down. The handful of strangers on the peninsula who had been logging at a leisurely pace soon found themselves surrounded by crews of men cutting down trees, setting up mills, and hauling logs or lumber out with team after team of oxen.

The peninsula gold rush to the redwood forests had begun. Contrary to the rumors current at the time, the forest land was not govern-ment land. Much of it was owned by Californios, who sometimes had no slips of paper to prove it, were confused by the land measures the strangers used when leasing or buying it, and were accustomed to dealing in hides rather than dollars or bartering today's favor into tomorrow's obligation. Frequently their land was stripped of timber by the time they had defended their title to it through the U.S. Board of Land Commissioners and the courts. Few took legal action against the timber thieves, either because they did not understand their rights or because they were intimidated by the hard-eyed men who acted as if they were the law.

Disappointed gold seekers looked toward the peninsula and saw its booming lumber industry as a source of enormous profits, or at least as a job that would pay more than their labors in the gold fields. Some, like the founders of the Woodside Store, used their profits to finance other enterprises that would exist long after the mountains had been plucked bare. Others, like the founder of the Pioneer Store, served as shipping agents for the lumbermen, bought real estate, and encouraged the growth of towns around them. Still others saw the land itself as a quick source of profit, taking advantage of the Californios' confusion in the new economy to relieve them of their ranchos and resell or lease them at double or even triple their purchase price. Some bought the land to use as little more than storage depots for the herds of American beef cattle they drove overland to sell at inflated prices to a ravenous San Francisco. And some of them stayed on the land, planting it to potatoes to satisfy the needs of other men on the way to fortune. A few, like the Steeles, began to look further ahead and saw the land as their future. They built homes and barns and plowed fields and bred dairy stock.

The Californios withdrew their families to isolated pockets like Portolá Valley, or to the safety of communities like Half Moon Bay, where they could speak their own language and retain their own customs. Before the 1850's were over, the strangers on the peninsula were not the newcomers but the Californios.

4

Buelna's Roadhouse

BUELNA'S ROADHOUSE was built in 1852 to meet the needs of a small community of displaced Californios. Félix Buelna, *alcalde* (mayor) of San José for three terms, tried to accommodate himself to the customs of the strangers flooding into his homeland, even serving as marshal in 1849, but like many of his countrymen he eventually withdrew to the isolation of Portolá Valley, where his friend Maximo Martínez gave him 95 acres of land. Martínez, who was successful in defending the title to his rancho before the U.S. Board of Land Commissioners, allowed less fortunate Californios to use his land as a refuge. In Portolá Valley, the new Yankee ordinances prohibiting Sunday gambling, bear and bull fighting, and other recreations traditional to the Californios were not valid. Here, along an old trail (now Alpine Road), Buelna built his roadhouse, providing himself with a living and his countrymen with a place to play *monte* or to dance.

A grandson of Félix Buelna says he lost all of his property in a poker game, and a scrap of paper bearing his signature and a few words in barely legible Spanish seems to bear him out. Three entries dated in October and November of 1868 acknowledge token payments for Buelna's land and roadhouse. The name of the witness to the property transfer filed in the county records is that of Moses Davis, a Searsville saloonkeeper well-known for running crooked card games. Buelna left the area soon after, and his roadhouse gradually ceased to be the exclusive gathering place for Californios.

William Eccles Stanton was only twenty years old when he acquired Buelna's roadhouse and land. For the next few years he leased it, but when he married in 1875 Stanton took over the management himself. Stanton's Saloon, as it then was called, stayed in the Stanton family until 1941, but after Stanton's death under the wheels of a train in 1887 the saloon was managed by a variety of colorful characters.

An immigrant from the Azores, F. Rodriguez Crovello, or Black Chapete, as he liked to be called, had the longest and most turbulent tenure. Black Chapete was regarded by his customers as a likable, easy-going bachelor who drank up much of his profits, but less tolerant citizens accused him of running a place that had "the reputation of being vile even for a roadhouse." The opening of Stanford University in 1891 brought Black Chapete a steady supply of new customers and some headaches as well. Disturbed by the obvious familiarity of their students with Black Chapete's establishment, University officials pressured the State of California to fine him for operating without a license, and for any other infractions that could be proved. Black Chapete paid his fine, and thereafter avoided serving minors over the bar by taking their drinks to them outside.

At the turn of the century, the small community of Mayfield (now part of Palo Alto) had more than twenty saloons. Stanford administrators battled for a decade to close these threats to student morality, succeeding in the winter of 1904, only

Buelna's Roadhouse, 1906

to have most of them open again just across the line in San Mateo County, where the Board of Supervisors, many of them saloonkeepers themselves, were more hospitable. Charlie Wright, one of the out-of-work Mayfield barkeeps, joined in partnership with Black Chapete. By the terms of a new lease with Mrs. Stanton for the princely sum of $35 a month, she agreed to give the building its first coat of paint.

Buelna's Roadhouse, 1975

State laws passed in 1909 prohibiting liquor sales within a mile and a half of a college campus closed down competitors in Menlo Park and left Chapete untouched. But insobriety, time, and an easy-going nature took their toll. In November of 1911, the Redwood City *Democrat* noted "Rodriquez Crovello, the 'Chapita' of old, who caused the county authorities countless troubles by his manner of conducting his saloon on the Portolá Road, has gone to the poor farm."

During World War I another "dry zone," around Menlo Park's Camp Fremont, just missed Buelna's Roadhouse, and for a while soldiers became the saloon's economic mainstay. But the nationwide dry zone imposed by the Eighteenth Amendment included, officially at least, the roadhouse. Julius Schenkel, the current lessee, renamed the place Schenkel's Picnic Park and continued to assuage the thirst of picnickers, campers, and his regulars. Soft drinks were sold openly, but more substantial refreshments were usually available on request. When the exuberant parties of students following the repeal of Prohibition drove Schenkel to retirement, the saloon was leased and later purchased by Enrico Rossotti, who renamed it Rossotti's (as it is still known to many of its patrons).

In 1957 John R. Alexander and Donald D. Hortner leased and then bought the old roadhouse, renamed it the Alpine Inn, tore out the interior partitions, and moved the bar to one side. The exterior has changed very little since 1852: lean-tos have been built on and removed, the façade has had a cornice with decorative brackets added, and posts have been installed to support the veranda roof. That so few of its proprietors have chosen to alter it is surely a tribute to the functional simplicity of Félix Buelna's original structure. He and Black Chapete probably shared a chuckle when their old roadhouse was declared a State Landmark in 1969, and placed on the National Register of Historic Places in August 1973.

Johnston Brothers Ranches

THE PRESENCE of a nearby Spanish-speaking community in Half Moon Bay may have been one of the reasons James Johnston, owner of San Francisco's infamous El Dorado Saloon, chose to buy land there. In 1852 Johnston married Petra María Jara, a recent immigrant from Chile. He also was looking for convenient range land for the herd of 800 cattle his brothers were driving out from the East. Late in 1853, soon after the herd arrived, the Johnstons built a house on the Half Moon Bay ranch, but James did not move his wife and family into it until 1855 or 1856.

James Johnston's house, now only a boarded-up shell, was built in the saltbox form familiar to New Englanders. The lower end of the sloping gallery that gives the characteristic saltbox form has been lost, probably in the 1906 earthquake. Many romantic stories are told about the luxurious life led by Petra and James in their house

William Johnston's House

James Johnston's House

near Half Moon Bay, but Petra lived there only six years before her death in 1861, and afterward James lived in San Francisco, returning only occasionally to visit his three sons, who were raised by Petra's mother and James's unmarried sister Isabella. In the depression of the 1870's, James lost many of his real estate holdings, including most of the ranch at Half Moon Bay. After 1885 the house was occupied by a man who cultivated the remaining 420 acres on shares. Soon afterward the house began its slide toward its present derelict appearance.

In 1854 William Johnston built a house for his family on land he bought adjoining his brother's ranch. William used the locally popular interpretation of classical style for his house, employing the same type of pegged frame construction used in James's house. A sensible innovation for protection from the coastal winds was to place the main entrance in the single-story wing attached to the back of the two-story rectangle. The elab-

7

Doorway of William Johnston's House

orate window cornices and ornate eave brackets typical of the style can still be seen, but the only remaining section of a veranda-like porch across the front of the one-story wing is over the door.

William Johnston became a popular member of the community, serving for years as a trustee of the local school board. He was active in civic affairs and in the local Methodist church. When people in the area referred to the Johnston place, they usually meant William's house, not James's. William and his family lived in their house well into this century. It was kept painted and in good repair until the mid-1960's, when it was sold to Westinghouse Corporation, which uses it to house farm workers. Now many of the original shutters have fallen off, its paint is worn thin by the punishing salt winds, and deterioration seems to be progressing rapidly.

8

Woodside Store

THE WOODSIDE STORE is the only survivor of several stores that served the loggers on the bay side of the redwood forests. It did not become the nucleus of a town in those days because the owners refused to sell any of the land around it, but almost from its beginning it served as a post office and gathering place for the men working in the nearby sawmills. The store was built, as one might expect, entirely of local redwood, a vertical board-and-batten sheath over a wooden frame. Several additions have been made since it was originally built in 1854. There is now a decided slant to the floor of the main room, but considering that the building has no foundation other than redwood sills and was built over a creek, its state of preservation comments well on the virtues of redwood construction.

Mathias Parkhurst and Robert Tripp, founders of the store, came to the Woodside area, each with another partner, in 1849. All four men were splitting shingles when Parkhurst's partner decided to try his luck in the gold fields. The remaining trio then joined together in a lucrative venture to provide piles for new docks in San Francisco. The logs were dragged by teams of oxen to the nearest tidewater slough on the bay, lashed together into rafts, and floated north to San Francisco by tide action. The slough became known, not surprisingly, as Redwood Creek, and the community that developed next to it as Redwood City.

The third partner, a man named Ryder, returned to Massachusetts after a severe mauling by a grizzly bear. Not long after, in 1851, Parkhurst came up with the idea of selling general merchandise out of the tiny two-room shack in which he and Tripp were living. The venture was an immediate success, and in less than three years the partners built a new and larger store across the road and began to dispense the numerous services expected of a country store. Tripp, who had studied dentistry in Philadelphia, could be summoned to provide emergency dental care, but most of the time he managed the ranch Parkhurst had purchased in 1849.

Besides running a post office, a general store, and a dental office, Parkhurst served drinks (without benefit of a license) from a barrel of whiskey on the counter, kept ostensibly to ease the pain of Tripp's patients. The first round was free; later rounds required a "contribution." After 1859 the store also housed the newly formed Woodside Library Association's collection of some 500 volumes.

Parkhurst died at the young age of 34, and when his estate was settled in 1868 Tripp acquired his land and the Woodside Store. By then San Francisco's insatiable appetite for lumber had nearly denuded the eastern slopes of the mountains, and the mills had moved over the crest to the coastside. But much of the lumber continued to be hauled back over the mountains to Redwood City. The Woodside Store was strategically located at the foot of King's Mountain Road, and many a teamster dropped in to steady his nerves after descending the steep grade, and to

Doc and Addie Tripp with Woodside Store customers, ca. 1890

9

Woodside Store, 1975

pick up mail and supplies for the men in the mills on his return trip.

Gradually, as the lumber industry began to decline all over the peninsula, the Woodside Store's customers were more likely to be farmers than lumbermen. In 1907 Tripp considered retiring, but the store was not closed until his death in 1909 at the age of 93. His only daughter sold the stock and locked the doors. At her death in 1926 the store was left to the Woodside Community Church. In 1940 the Woodside Store became the first historic building to be purchased by the County of San Mateo.

Pioneer Store

THE PIONEER STORE is one of the few remaining examples of the brick, one-story commercial structure so common in the 1850's in northern California. Because in 1859 the business interests of its builder, John Vogan Diller, were directed toward both the street in front and Redwood Creek in back, the structure was given two identical façades. The modified classical detailing often used on public buildings has resulted here in a sense of simple dignity. Directly beneath the main cornice there is a simple classical entablature with a strong dentil course. Both back and front façades featured three arches between four quasi-Doric pilasters. The central and somewhat larger arch accommodated double doors under a fan light, and the side arches, also topped by fan lights, added a touch of elegance by the use of casement windows. All windows and doors were protected by 1/4-inch cast-iron shutters.

When Diller first located on the *embarcadero* in 1853, he and about 150 other people were taking a chance on being promptly dispossessed. A rumor had started that the Argüello claim to the Rancho de las Pulgas would not be validated. Squatters began to pour into the ranch, creating in a few weeks a raucus, unruly boom town adjacent to the landing. With as many as 50 teamloads of lumber a day being hauled into it for transshipment, the site was clearly one with a prosperous future.

When the title was cleared in 1853, the Argüellos' attorney, Simón Monserrate Mezes, was given the *embarcadero* area as his fee. Mezes at once hired a surveyor to plot a town along Redwood Creek, ignoring the homes and businesses that had already been built by the squatters. When he advertised the lots for sale at $75 each, most of the squatters chose to pay rather than sacrifice their advantageous position or their improvements. When the town was incorporated in 1867, the citizens took their revenge by rejecting the name on the original plot map, Mezesville, and giving it the name in current usage, Redwood City.

Diller's own location was excellent. Through his back door he operated as a shipping agent for the lumbermen in the mountains, and through his front door he carried on his mercantile trade. By 1869, when Diller's other business and civic interests had become extensive, he sold his share of the business to a partner he had taken on three years before.

Philander Peregrine Chamberlain, the next owner of the Pioneer Store building, came to Redwood City in 1868 and soon became one of the town's leading citizens. The Pioneer Store with its pot-bellied stove (reputed to be the largest in town) was a popular meeting place for catching up on community news. And Chamberlain was certainly a popular man. It was said that at one time or another just about everyone in the county owed him money, but he never sent bills. He claimed that over his lifetime in business he had lost very little by extending credit.

Chamberlain took his civic responsibilities seriously. He was elected San Mateo County

Pioneer Store as it was

Pioneer Store, 1975

Treasurer in 1882 and served in that capacity without interruption until failing health forced his retirement in 1925. During many of these 43 years of service, the Pioneer Store was also in the county's service. San Mateo County's big iron safe sat in the back of the store protecting the county's funds. Public officials deemed the sturdily constructed Pioneer Store a safer repository than the County Court House.

Their evaluation was justified when the building came through the 1906 earthquake with minor damage. A parapet had to be replaced and a sign was knocked askew, but the store was soon back to normal. In fact, better than normal, since the brick walls were cleaned and the trim re-painted in the repair process.

In 1916 the mercantile life of the Pioneer Store came to a close. It served as a classroom for an aviation school during World War I and as a garage in the 1920's; it is currently a laundry. The present state of the building is unfortunate. The front has been modernized by bricking in two of the three graceful arches, and the century-old bricks are covered by a coat of scaling pink paint. The back of the building has been less dramatically altered, retaining both of its side windows and their iron shutters.

White House

MARINERS coming up the coast of California in the middle of the last century kept watch for the White House, a lonely landmark on the south coast of the peninsula by which they reckoned the distance left to San Francisco. Isaac Graham, the owner of that house, was a tall, aggressive mountain man who swaggered through the closing days of the Mexican period in California, and cut a somewhat smaller figure during the early years of statehood. He has been described as being lawless and quarrelsome and unabashedly crude, and for all his litigation, astute investment, and wealth, he could neither read nor write. Graham was also a courageous man, a natural leader, and he was used to handling firearms.

While operating a still and a saloon in the Salinas area in 1836, Graham recruited a company of riflemen from the foreign trappers, runaway sailors, and woodsmen in the area to fight for Juan Bautista Alvarado and José Castro in their revolt against an appointed Mexican governor. The bragging of Graham and his followers about their contribution became so obstreperous, however, that in 1840 the new governor, fearing a rumored counterrevolution, rounded up many foreigners and deported them to Mexico. When they were released, with apologies and an indemnity from the government of Mexico, Graham was one of the few who chose to return to California.

Graham bought land near Zayante in Santa Cruz County, set up another still and a grist mill, did some tanning, and put into operation the first water-powered sawmill in California. By the 1850's, he was reputed to be one of the wealthiest men in Santa Cruz County. In 1851 he bought Rancho Punta de Año Nuevo to provide winter range for his cattle and a job for his son Wayne. The son did not accept the offer and the ranch was leased out. Not long after this, the old house on it burned.

The house was replaced with a two-story white frame building set on a hill commanding a fine view of the sea. Even though Graham probably had little to do with the building of the house and certainly spent little time there, it was known locally as Captain Graham's house or the Graham house, but to the sailors and their captains it was known simply as the White House, the landmark that told them San Francisco was coming up soon.

The White House is a simple, unassuming farmhouse, typical of the houses built by Americans as they moved west. A kitchen or service wing extends out to the right of the main rectangle of the building, and both wings are sheathed with horizontal redwood clapboards. The window frames have the only distinctive style element, which may, incidentally, have led to the

Tenants added a Mexican oven

tradition that they were "brought around the Horn." They have a flattened cornice, which is a simple form of Italianate style popular in the 1850's. Whatever the source of the window frames, Isaac Graham's house had for some years the reputation of being the finest house of the south coast.

In time, Graham encumbered the Año Nuevo ranch with a high-interest mortgage, and when he was unable to raise the money to stay foreclosure in 1862, it was sold at auction. Six months later the buyer sold it at a $10,000 profit to Jeremiah T. Clarke and his brother-in-law, Loren Coburn. The purchasers had arranged a tentative lease with purchase options with the Steele Brothers corporation even before the sale was final.

In 1880 after a series of ownership changes, the White House was moved from its imposing site to make room for the grander house of Rensselaer Steele's daughter. The house was not razed, however, and has been almost continuously occupied since it was first built.

This house was destroyed by fire in February 1976, after the type for this book was set.

14

Steele Brothers Dairies

The first Steele Brothers Dairy was established in Marin County on the remote Rancho Punta de los Reyes. It began almost by chance when Clara, the wife of Rensselaer Steele, included a couple of rounds of her cheese in the wagonload of farm produce going to San Francisco from their rented farm. The response was immediate: San Francisco would take as much as she could send. Within five years Rensselaer and his three cousins (incorporated under the name of Steele Brothers) had a herd of 600 dairy cows and were in the market for additional land. They found it in the hands of the new owners of Isaac Graham's Rancho Punta de Año Nuevo and the Rancho Butaño. It was beautiful rich land, well watered by creeks and springs. There were some who warned that only the tough Californio breed of cattle could survive on the windswept, fog-ridden plains of California's coast, but the Steeles had proven the fallacy of that old myth on similar land in Marin County. On the last day of 1862, the Steeles' first shipment of cattle left Marin County by boat for the south coast ranches.

Cascade Ranch Dairy Building

Cascade Ranch Dairy Building

The Steeles were resourceful people, with many talents among them. To provide lumber for their buildings, Rensselaer set up a sawmill in the redwoods in Cascade Canyon. The first building to go up in 1862 was the dairy building. This structure was designed with an eye to function rather than style, which may explain the irregular placement of windows. The building has three floors but only two exits. The presence of two brick chimneys and the fact that the walls were insulated with sawdust suggest that Mrs. Steele's cheese was of the variety that required an even and slightly elevated temperature. The wide band, or fascia, just under the eaves was the builder's one architectural embellishment.

Cascade Ranch House

Cascade Ranch House

The most elegant building constructed during the Steeles' years on the peninsula was the home built for Rensselaer and Clara Steele. Sketch plans for it were found among the papers of Isaac Steele, who was the group's most skilled builder. Elements of the restrained classic forms familiar

Cloverdale Ranch Barn

Details of unusual roof bracing

to the Steeles in their years in New York and Ohio must have made their isolated ranch seem more homelike. A wide veranda with a balcony on the second floor ran along the front and both sides of the house. The balcony was supported across the front by six Tuscan pillars set in distinct pairs and echoed in the balustrade. The placement of doors and windows on the first floor was repeated on the second, although in recent years picture windows have been added to the lower story. The original windows had shutters. Side chimneys at each end of the simple gable roof served fireplaces in the major rooms on

16

both floors. The sophisticated fascia used under the eaves of the nearby dairy building was applied here more appropriately. A wing was added to the rear of the house in 1884. The ugly flat-roofed extensions on each side of the building were added more recently. There have also been alterations in the interior, but the symmetrical floor plan and its straight-run staircase have survived.

Cloverdale Ranch Barn

This barn was built in 1863 by an experienced craftsman, influenced by barns he either recalled or helped to build in the eastern United States. Unlike the usual California barn, with its long, sloping roof, this one enclosed its space by going up three stories, reducing the roof size and maintenance cost without losing square footage. The enormous foot-square beams and uprights were joined together in a tenon-and-mortise technique with pegs of locust wood an inch in diameter.

An ingenious bracing of roof timbers spreads the weight evenly over its supports.

The barn has three aisles of more or less equal width. Fodder bins line the center aisle on either side of a wooden track along which carts were pulled to haul feed to the stanchions. Each side aisle had stanchions for thirty-six cows. The upper floors of the barn were used to store hay.

Care in construction is evident throughout. The dowels must have been well seasoned, for they are still snug in their holes. The thick redwood floor slabs were fitted tightly, and remain so even today.

Ramsey-Steele House

The Steeles' Cloverdale Ranch belonged briefly to a man named William F. Ramsey, who built a modest but very fashionable house on it in 1873. It is a two-story house in Classical Revival style, with three rooms on each floor. An interior chimney serves two back-to-back fireplaces. The outer

Ramsey-Steele House

Details. Bay window and quoins

17

Dickerman Barn

Dickerman Barn

Isaac Steele's daughter Effie and her husband, Edwin Dickerman, built their home and dairy buildings near Año Nuevo Creek. The barn makes use of construction methods similar to those used in the larger Cloverdale Ranch barn, but the beams used are even larger, 18 x 18 inches. They were salvaged after 1877 from a burned-out wharf in nearby Año Nuevo Cove. The buildings are now owned by the California State Department of Parks and Recreation.

Año Nuevo Ranch House

An interesting example of the New England saltbox form is Horace Steele's Año Nuevo Ranch House, built in 1895 across from his father's Green Oaks Ranch. Here the house is placed with its back to the coast winds. The style did not prevent the builders from adding innovations, however, notably the polygonal bay window on the south side. The house is occupied today by Steele's youngest daughter.

Año Nuevo Ranch House

support of each stair end of the graceful stairway leading to the second floor is decorated with a scroll design, and a dainty balustrade curves into the turned newel post.

The main portion of the house is formed by two intersecting rectangles, with a single-story service room on the back. Quoins have been used to decorate the corners of the exterior walls, and the gables end in raking cornices. The most elegant flourish of the house is in its flat-roofed, polygonal bay window, displaying delicate dentil brackets under the cornice and flat, recessed Italianate panels above each window. Although four-over-four windows are used elsewhere in the house, the bay has large-paned double-hung windows. The main entry, protected until recently by an added-on porch, is graced by a horizontal glass transom and narrow side lights. In 1896 the service wing was lengthened with salvaged lumber.

The house was occupied until 1974, when it was sold to Campbell Soup Company.

Chapter Two

Coastside Communities
1860's-1900's

THE SINGLE most striking feature of the San Francisco Peninsula is its geography. A crescent-shaped ridge of mountains, the romantic Sierra Morena or prosaic Outer Coast Range, divides the peninsula socially, economically, and climatically. On the warm, dry bayside, people moved freely over the plains with little more than an occasional creek to ford, and their ships were safe in the tidal sloughs of the bay. Not so on the coastside, caught in the enclosing grasp of the curve of the mountains. Here the hills seemed to catch the wind and fog off the Pacific and roll them back onto the land. The narrow, fertile valleys were divided from one another by ridges, sometimes rough, sometimes rolling, but always making travel difficult. On the north the crescent was closed by the forbidding San Pedro Mountain and on the south by precipitous chalk bluffs on an active fault. And the coast with its steep cliffs and treacherous reefs provided no easy alternative means of transportation for men or goods.

During the Spanish and Mexican periods in California, the coastside was left almost entirely to the Indian population, who lived well on the abundance of fish and wildlife. In 1846, however, when the Bear Flag Revolution visited its cruelties on the Californio population of the San Francisco Bay area, two large families moved with their sons and daughters and their families to adjoining coastal ranchos. A number of adobes were built to house them on the banks of Pilarcitos Creek. Other Californios soon followed, and the little

town they called San Benito was formed. Their isolation was short-lived as foreigners in search of land arrived. And following them were the men who opened general stores, blacksmith shops, saloons, and all the other businesses that followed the American settler. These latecomers dubbed the predominantly Californio settlement at San Benito Spanishtown. Later, as the foreign population began to outnumber the first settlers, the town became known as Half Moon Bay.

In time each of the narrow little valleys formed

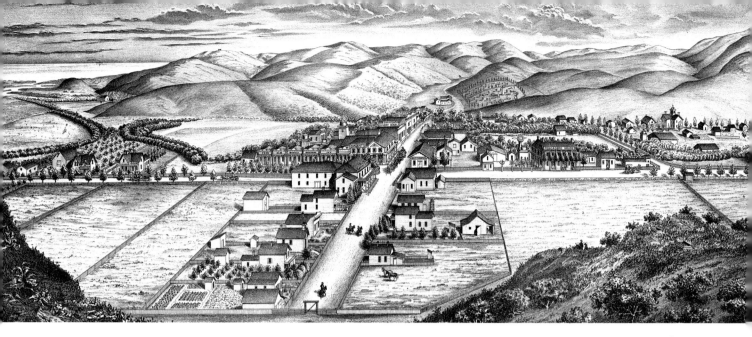

*Pescadero, 1878. San Gregorio Street runs vertically through the picture.
On its right the Thomas W. Moore House and the I.O.O.F. Hall can
be identified. On the left is the Garretson Schoolhouse. The Braddock
Weeks House is on the far right, and the first St. Anthony's Church is
on the uppermost street on the right.*

by the creeks rushing from the mountains to the sea had a sign of civilization—a farm, a general store, a saloon, or, after the stage roads were graded over the mountains from San Mateo and Redwood City, a resort hotel. Where hamlets or villages developed, however, they served primarily the local farmers and dairymen.

The rich Pescadero Valley was once described as one large potato patch by a traveler, but to San Franciscans the names Pescadero and San Gregorio brought visions of resort hotels and happy days spent exploring beaches and redwood groves.

The coastside of the peninsula had its share of lumber-producing forests, but economically they had little effect on most residents. The loggers worked their way up from the bayside, but even after they moved over the crest of the mountains, they typically hauled the lumber back over the paths they had cleared to bay ports for easier shipment. This lack of a safe port was the main obstacle to the development of the coastside, and the settlers there tried many inventive solutions to the problem of getting their produce, be it cheese, potatoes, or shingles, to market. They built enormous chutes, rigged hawsers and slings from high cliffs, and built a wharf 700 feet over

the surf to deep water. Needless to say, ship-owners were still reluctant to risk their ships and crews so close to the dangerous reefs along the coast, and the cost of shipment remained high.

For many on the coastside, the hope was a railroad. Sooner or later, they believed, the physical obstacles would be overcome and they would be able to get their produce to market as quickly as their competitors on the bayside. The railroad was a long time coming because the cost over such rough terrain was too high for the revenue anticipated. To further complicate matters, the 1906 earthquake undid much of the grading and tossed some of the expensive equipment that had been used into the sea. The tracks, one starting in Santa Cruz and the other in San Francisco, never were joined, and the temporarily profitable link at the southern end was driven out of business by one of the Southern Pacific's stratagems. By then the truck and the passenger car had taken over many of the railroad's functions.

These obstacles to development may be one of the reasons the coastside has so many examples of the buildings of early settlers. The damp, salty fog and the hard winds of the Pacific are well known for their destructiveness to the works of man, but they are not nearly as destructive as the bulldozer.

22

PESCADERO

PESCADERO means fishing place in Spanish. The village is said to have been given its name by Spanish settlers who noted that it was a favored fishing spot for the local Indians. From Pescadero's earliest days, people have noted an architectural unity in the community that set it off from other villages. This unity is still in evidence today, even though many of its more distinctive buildings have been destroyed by fire. The origin of Pescadero's style is not easy to identify. An unusual number of the original settlers came from Maine, and they may have brought with them fairly strong ideas about the proper appearance of a village. The relative isolation of the Pescadero Valley (electricity did not arrive until 1925) may have kept their ideas from being diluted by innovations from outside. There cannot have been many carpenters in the area, and their notion of a well-built house undoubtedly limited the variety of styles in their neighborhood. Or the unity of style may simply have resulted from the effect on newcomers of a few particularly pleasing houses already in the community.

Pescadero's resemblance to a trim New England village has lessened considerably in recent years, but unlike most of the peninsula's bayside residents a large percentage of Pescadero's population is descended from its original founders. It is still a quiet village; the population has never been more than a few hundred.

Alexander Moore House

IN 1853 Alexander Moore and his brother Thomas moved to Pescadero Valley to farm the land their father had bought in 1852 from Juan José González. Alexander built a large fourteen-room house for his wife and six children northeast of the present site of the village. Designed along vaguely classical lines in Greek Revival style, this dignified country home may well have been the model by which subsequent buildings were judged. The pierced columns of its porch appeared again and again in the community in many variations. When the house burned in January 1975, much of the original redwood plank flooring was still intact, and it rested on the original redwood sills. Although sagging a bit from the inevitable settling of a century and a quarter, it had the general appearance of a substantial, attractive farmhouse.

The Alexander Moore House as reconstructed from old photographs

Braddock Weeks House

BRADDOCK WEEKS and his wife were both born and raised in Maine. Weeks owned part interest in Pescadero's first store, but his initial income came from the 100 acres he planted to potatoes. The hunger for "Irish oranges" in San Francisco seemed insatiable, and potatoes were more easily transported and less perishable than many crops that could be grown in the area.

The house Weeks built in the 1860's displays many of the traditional components of Pescadero houses. The pierced columns first seen on the Alexander Moore House are there, but extra bosses were added in the centers and fancily cut ornaments at the tops. Decorative brackets are used under the long eaves as well as at the gable ends. The main entry is topped by a transom light with long, thin side lights. Window frames have Italianate cornices.

San Gregorio Street

BY 1860 Pescadero had most of the basic structures for a proper village: a store, a post office, a hotel, and a schoolhouse. Saloons and churches were soon to follow. The business district developed around the intersection of the stage road (San Gregorio Street) and Ocean Road (Pescadero Creek Road). There were general stores, butcher shops, saloons, livery stables, two hotels, and a blacksmith shop. The presence of two hotels in such a small village arose from the area's reputation for good hunting and good fishing, and later as a place from which to explore the redwood country or Pescadero's Pebble Beach. For all its resort attractions, however, Pescadero remained firmly oriented toward its farmland.

Fire has been more cruel than time to the old buildings of Pescadero. Fires taking a single building are common in isolated communities, but in 1921 most of the northwest side of San Gregorio Street was destroyed by fire, and in 1926 an even more devastating fire leveled the northeast side. Less than a year later the town's largest and oldest hotel, the Swanton House, was burnt to the ground along with its guest cottages. By 1975 all that remained of the old downtown district were scattered structures on the two ends of San Gregorio Street.

master craftsman in its redwood truss construction. Natural redwood has been left throughout and much of the original hardware is in evidence. To accommodate a modern restroom a smaller lancet window was added to the front, producing an unbalanced façade. A spire has been removed from the bell tower.

Methodist-Episcopal Church

Methodist-Episcopal Church

The Methodist-Episcopal Church was built next to the I.O.O.F. Hall in 1890. By 1905 the local Methodist membership could no longer afford to support a pastor and sold the church. It was used as a community social center in the 1920's and as a Japanese cultural center until the end of 1941, and is currently owned by the Native Sons and Native Daughters of the Golden West. Designed on a cruciform plan, the building has some Gothic Revival details and a high-pitched roof. The open ceiling reveals the work of a

San Gregorio Street

I.O.O.F. Hall

I.O.O.F. Hall

In 1874 a chapter of the International Order of Odd Fellows was organized, and soon became one of the most active fraternal groups in the area. In 1875 it purchased the Mt. Hope Cemetery, and in 1878 it bought property on San Gregorio Street for an I.O.O.F. hall. An addition to the front of the building produced its present rectangular shape. In 1890 the street façade was made more elaborate by adding an overhang to the gable and installing decorative brackets under the eaves. A veranda was attached with a balustraded balcony. In recent years the building has been used as a private residence. Mismatched windows on the front have destroyed its classic symmetry, and an incongruous two-car garage has been added to one side.

San Gregorio Street: I.O.O.F. Hall, Woodhams House, Thomas W. Moore House

Woodhams House

The Woodhams House was not built until the mid-1890's, when Aldred Winfred Woodhams and his bride moved to Pescadero to open a butcher shop. The house has the square bay window common to the 1880's, but it is the decorative detail that gives it interest. Pierced quarter-fan ornaments appear on each corner of the porch and on either side of the supports. In the apex of the gable there is a simple stick form and at the crest a double fan with a finial center. Sections remain of the delicate lacy cresting on the gable ridge.

Thomas W. Moore House

Fortunately, the Thomas W. Moore House, built by Alexander Moore's younger brother, is on the block spared by the fires. The house was probably built around 1863, when Thomas married, and it shows the architectural influence of his older brother's house. Although a narrow town lot dictated the elongated shape, the same classically inspired motifs were used. Here the pierced columns support a balustrade. A few of the original louvered shutters cling precariously to the upper windows. The single-story kitchen wing at the back was probably part of the original construction, since it appears in the 1878 lithograph on page 22.

Woodhams House

Thomas W. Moore House

James McCormick House

AT THE opposite end of San Gregorio Street, on the south bank of Pescadero Creek, is the house James McCormick built in the late 1860's. James was one of four brothers and three sisters who migrated from their native Ireland to New York and then to California. In the Pescadero area James did some farming, bought into several businesses, and acquired large timber holdings.

Architecturally, the McCormick House is the most sophisticated of the houses built in the 1860's in Pescadero. Influenced by the Classical Revival, the house is almost a mirror image of the Thomas W. Moore House on the other end of San Gregorio Street. It has the same window arrangement, although it uses four panes in each section rather than six as in the Moore House. The louvered shutters are the same, but the transom light over the door is larger and accompanied by narrow side lights. The detail of the front door is more elaborate in that all four panels are in the shape of octagons. The surface of the siding is regularly scored to give it the appearance of stone. The veranda pillars are substantial square supports whose panels are as interesting for their shadows and depth as the pierced columns used in other Pescadero houses. The porch also extends along the side, a luxury the narrower lot of the Moore House would not allow.

Congregational Church

THE Congregational Church directly across the street from the James McCormick House was built in 1867. It is the oldest church surviving on its original site on the San Francisco Peninsula. It began as a simple frame church about 34 x 54 feet in area, with a square, louvered bell tower above the entry. The church expresses in wood the temple forms of Classical Revival: cornice returns, quoins, and a complete entablature. The semicircular, segmented transom light over the entry is repeated above the double-hung windows

Interior and side view

Congregational Church

along the side of the building. The bell tower has a pseudo-rose window in the shape of a Maltese cross. The siding, as in the McCormick House across the street, is scored to simulate stone, but here the imitation of stone is carried further by the use of quoins.

In 1889 John F. Wilson drew up plans for the forty-foot shingle-covered Victorian Gothic spire atop the square bell tower. At the same time the choir loft was moved from the rear of the sanctuary to behind the pulpit, foundation repairs were made, and the lot was fenced. More recently a modern kitchen and classroom were added to the back.

29

Bartlett V. Weeks House

Concave fan

THERE WERE three men named Weeks living in Pescadero in the nineteenth century, all from Kennebec County, Maine, and none related to either of the others. One of them, Bartlett V. Weeks, bought 157 acres from Juan José González in 1860 and moved with his family into the old González home north of Pescadero Creek.

In 1885 Weeks built a wooden frame house next to the adobe on what is now called Goulson Road. The house showed a new if conservative departure from the older Pescadero model in that it demonstrated an awareness of the Victorian style and omitted some of the typical style components in Pescadero. The porch columns were not pierced, for instance, and the double-hung windows were glazed with single panes and had no shutters. The main entry to the house is in the back ell, well protected from the wind. The veranda once stretched around three sides of the house, and its columns were decorated by concave fans that suggest arches between the posts. The house is currently occupied by the third generation of the Weeks family.

Garretson Schoolhouse

In 1875, because of some dissatisfaction with the public school, John Garretson built his own private schoolhouse. It appears as the fourth building from the bottom in the lithograph on page 22. The building was a simple little box, but the gable brackets gave it a certain distinction. Mr. Garretson's schoolhouse had a fairly brief life as a school, for in 1885 it was purchased by Braddock Weeks and moved to its present area to serve as his dairy building. Structurally, it appears to be little changed, except for the loss of its tiny bell tower and the substitution of a stovepipe for the brick chimney once at its back. The schoolhouse shares with a similar one-room school in San Gregorio the distinction of being the earliest surviving elementary school on the San Francisco Peninsula.

Garretson Schoolhouse

St. Anthony's Church

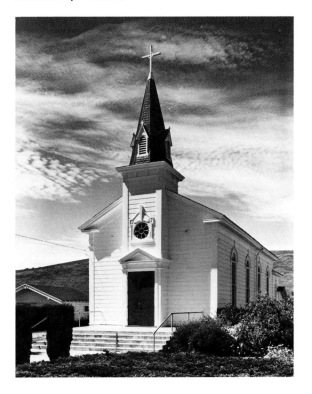

St. Anthony's Church

Pescadero in general suffered very little from the 1906 earthquake, but its neat little Catholic Church was shaken off its foundation and had to be razed. The building erected on its site is very much in keeping with the homes of the community, and similar in design to the Congregational Church. The style is basically Classical Revival, but the spire shows a strong Gothic influence. The spire is octagonal, cut by four pointed dormers with louver-filled arches and a small cross at each apex. The tower on which it rests has a rose window in a formal frame, glazed in a simple petal pattern. The side windows of the church are arched with hood molds topped by small crosses. Above the main entrance is a classical pediment.

San Gregorio House

BY THE TIME it reaches the Pacific, San Gregorio Creek has drained the waters from five mountain streams and passed through one of the coastside's most fertile valleys. In 1865, when Pescadero was already a prosperous village, George Washington Tully Carter paced off and bought five lonely acres on the northern bank of San Gregorio Creek near the stage road. The following year he advertised the opening of his San Gregorio House as a "summer resort for the citizens of San Francisco." Carter's hotel consisted of the southernmost three bays of today's San Gregorio House.

The son of a schoolteacher, Carter often wrote items of local interest for the *San Mateo County Gazette*, and occasionally included laments about the lonesomeness of running the only business in San Gregorio. Nonetheless, he assured his readers, San Gregorio was bound to be a metropolis one day. Carter stuck it out for three years, long enough to see San Gregorio develop from a mere stage stop to a busy hamlet. A general store opened down the road, then a saloon; by the 1870's a blacksmith shop, a butcher shop, a boot shop, a school, a post office, and a church had been added.

The hotel changed hands several times before John R. Evans bought it in 1875 and set about "tearing down and building up to suit the times." He added the seven bays on the north end and built a porch with a balustrade across the full front of the hotel. Surprisingly few changes have been made in the hundred intervening years. Many of the windows have their original glazing, the balustrade is original, and the four-paneled doors are unchanged. The eight-inch square posts supporting the veranda were replaced with logs that had been washed ashore, and the paint was changed from gray with white trim to brown with white trim.

In 1888 Evans sold the San Gregorio House to Jesse Palmer for $5,000 and some land Palmer owned in Redwood City. Palmer and his wife had lived for nearly twenty years in area lumber camps. In the winter of 1886, after four of their children died in a diphtheria epidemic, the couple took their surviving daughter and returned to England. But California had become their home, and they came back in 1888 to start a new life as hotelkeepers in San Gregorio. Palmer went into partnership with Frank Bell, who had been raised in the San Gregorio Valley, and in 1893 Bell married the Palmers' daughter.

For some passengers on the two stages that passed through San Gregorio, the hotel was only a pause for refreshment, but for many it was the reason for their journey. The trout fishing in San Gregorio was judged excellent. Guests were also attracted by the beach at the mouth of the creek, and by the hotel's excellent Chinese cook.

East elevation

San Gregorio House, 1975

The Palmers were proud of their self-sufficiency, doing their own butchering and curing of meat, raising their own vegetables and chickens, and making their own dairy products. They ran their own livery stable which sheltered 18 horses and offered a number of carriages for hire. Other miscellaneous buildings associated with the hotel included a granary, a water tower, a laundry house with a huge copper boiler embedded in a brick firebox, and an old dance hall with a makeshift stage. The Palmers later opened a saloon next to the hotel and converted it into a gas station during the Prohibition era.

The arrival of private passenger cars increased the San Gregorio House's clientele until the 1920's, when the community was bypassed by the new coast highway. In 1930 Mrs. Bell closed the hotel to guests but continued to live in it until her death. Today it is the home of her son, Frank Bell.

Pigeon Point Lighthouse

TRAVELERS along California's scenic Highway 1 are invariably excited when they first catch sight of the Pigeon Point Lighthouse. This classic building on an isolated cliff halfway between Santa Cruz and Half Moon Bay has been more often photographed and painted than any other light station on the West Coast. Built in 1871 of bricks manufactured on the site, the tower has withstood storms, earthquakes, and thus far the vagaries of human planners. It is the earliest lighthouse in California still functioning, and its priceless original French lens is still in place and still operable. Although fog on the peninsula's rugged coast has been the major threat to shipping, the light on Pigeon Point is also used by ships as a landfall light and an identification of the promontory at which coasting vessels make a course change.

Before the lighthouse was built and afterward until about 1900, Pigeon Point was the site of a fair-sized community of whalers and fishermen. It bore a number of names in its early years, but the one that became official originated, appropriately enough, from a shipwreck on its rocky reefs. The *Carrier Pigeon*, a clipper on her maiden voyage from Boston, came to grief there in a heavy

Aerial view, 1959. Keeper's Victorian house, built in 1872, has since been removed.

34

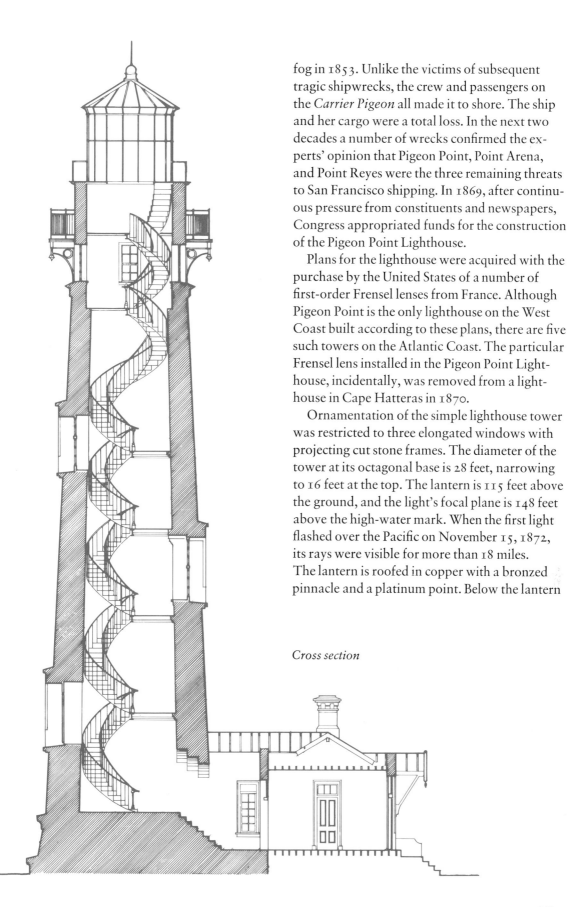

fog in 1853. Unlike the victims of subsequent tragic shipwrecks, the crew and passengers on the *Carrier Pigeon* all made it to shore. The ship and her cargo were a total loss. In the next two decades a number of wrecks confirmed the experts' opinion that Pigeon Point, Point Arena, and Point Reyes were the three remaining threats to San Francisco shipping. In 1869, after continuous pressure from constituents and newspapers, Congress appropriated funds for the construction of the Pigeon Point Lighthouse.

Plans for the lighthouse were acquired with the purchase by the United States of a number of first-order Frensel lenses from France. Although Pigeon Point is the only lighthouse on the West Coast built according to these plans, there are five such towers on the Atlantic Coast. The particular Frensel lens installed in the Pigeon Point Lighthouse, incidentally, was removed from a lighthouse in Cape Hatteras in 1870.

Ornamentation of the simple lighthouse tower was restricted to three elongated windows with projecting cut stone frames. The diameter of the tower at its octagonal base is 28 feet, narrowing to 16 feet at the top. The lantern is 115 feet above the ground, and the light's focal plane is 148 feet above the high-water mark. When the first light flashed over the Pacific on November 15, 1872, its rays were visible for more than 18 miles. The lantern is roofed in copper with a bronzed pinnacle and a platinum point. Below the lantern

Cross section

35

is a cantilevered iron gallery supported by sixteen elaborate cast-iron brackets.

The original lamp burned refined lard, which was eventually replaced by electricity. The chariot that pulled the lens apparatus around the lamp every four minutes was powered by a clock-type mechanism using 200-pound weights that had to be manually rewound every four hours. Even after this system was replaced by an electrical one, the clock mechanism was kept in working order for emergency use.

The small rectangular building attached to the base of the tower was known as the oil and work house and is now called the watch house. It is constructed of brick in a restrained Eastlake or

Watch house entrance

cottage style. The entrance is protected by a wooden canopy whose exposed braces are decorated with simple but distinctive stick detail. The braces are repeated in the gable. An interior hallway leads to a short flight of stairs and direct access to the tower. On each side of the hall there is one room containing a fireplace with a marble mantel.

For many years Pigeon Point had the most powerful light on the West Coast. The station was automated in 1974 with a modern aero beacon, but the original lens and lantern have been left in place. In many other West Coast lights these old lenses have been removed to museums, but Pigeon Point offers the interested visitor an example of a working lighthouse not only as it is today but as it was in the early days of California shipping. Perhaps one day this remarkable building will be open to the public.

Pablo Vásquez House and Stable

PABLO VÁSQUEZ was born at Mission Dolores in 1842, where his father served as *mayordomo* (government-appointed administrator of church property) from 1840 to 1846. His father moved the family to their Rancho el Corral de Tierra to protect them from the brutal incidents other Californios experienced in the Bear Flag revolt of 1846. Although the world around him was changing rapidly, Pablo Vásquez recalled his childhood in Half Moon Bay as one of much

Pablo Vásquez House

freedom, with wild horses to tame and open land to ride over. His skill and grace in the saddle were often commented on by those who had seen him flash by on the back of a palomino. He organized a racetrack south of town where local riders competed on Sundays. According to legend, Pablo Vásquez was also an expert billiard player who on more than one occasion posed as an inexperienced country boy and then outplayed his high-betting opponents.

Somewhat south of the adobe home built by his father, Pablo Vásquez had a one-story wooden frame house built in 1869. The style is an interpretation of late Greek Revival, and its most distinctive features are in the treatment of the entry and windows. The entrance is covered by a portico supported by square Tuscan pillars. A strong, pointed pediment is braced by delicate, paired brackets. The door itself has four unusual glazed panels. The flattened cornices over the windows are a reflection of the pediment over the portico.

The house is built in the shape of a long rectangle with an intersecting wing on the right side. All the interior walls and ceilings were of narrow redwood tongue-and-groove, but in the 1930's the living and dining rooms were plastered. A partition forming the narrow front hall was removed, creating a spacious front parlor.

Considering his ability with horses, it is not surprising that Pablo Vásquez should open a livery stable. His location at the edge of Half Moon Bay was convenient and allowed him to make use of the old Vásquez rancho corral. For a brief period in the 1880's Vásquez and a partner opened a stage line between Half Moon Bay and San Mateo, but the established line lowered its fares until their new rivals were forced to withdraw.

Pilarcitos Livery Stable was probably built sometime after the Vásquez house, but according to newspaper items some part of it was known to exist in 1872. Differences in siding suggest that it may have been built in stages as Vásquez's business interests changed.

Pilarcitos Livery Stable

Community Methodist Church

HALF MOON BAY has always been a predominantly Catholic town. Efforts to organize a Methodist-Episcopal church began as early as 1864, but until their building was erected in 1872 the Methodists of Half Moon Bay shared circuit-riding preachers with Pescadero. In 1872, largely through the generosity of Alexander Gordon, a man with extensive real estate holdings, the *San Mateo County Gazette* was able to announce that "Plans and specifications for the new Methodist Episcopal Church have been prepared by Mr. Charles Geddes, architect of San Francisco, and tenders have been called for the immediate erection of the building."

The style of architecture chosen for the church was Gothic Revival. The center of interest focused on the entry. Double doors and a segmented fanlight are set in a handsome ogival arch. The simple arch of each window is divided by mullions into two lancets and topped with a cross and the carved letter M. There is a small bull's-eye window in the gable. The eave brackets and the fascia are extremely plain. The belfry consists of an octagonal cupola with cut-out Victorian braces in the arch openings. Its roof is supported by a multitude of small but elaborate brackets. The bell is in full view.

According to newspaper accounts, the church was thrown off its foundations in the 1906 earthquake, but repairs were completed a little more than a year later. The building has been refurbished several times during the last century, most recently in 1975.

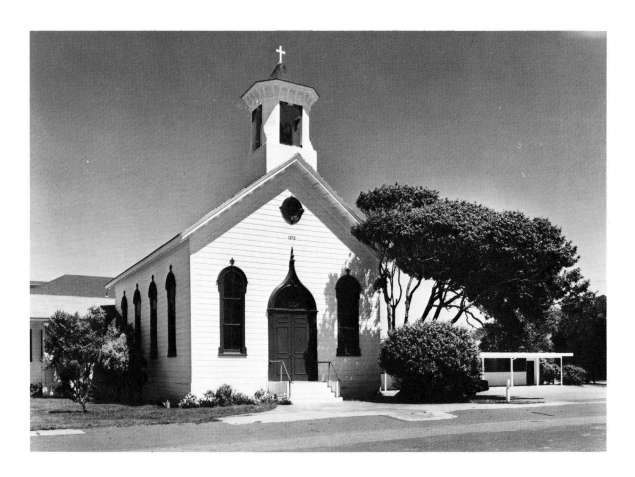

Chapter Three

Bayside Communities
1860's-1900's

In 1859 a journalist traveling by stagecoach down the bayside road El Camino Reál commented on seeing farms and orchards and windmills, but only one town. Redwood City then had a population of four or five hundred, he estimated. This peaceful rural scene attracted the eye of others besides passing journalists. In the next decade wealthy San Franciscans were buying estates up and down the peninsula. A few were speculating on the repeated rumors that a railroad would be built soon, but many others were simply looking for quiet places to build country houses. Summer homes were becoming fashionable, and San Francisco's cold, foggy summers added motivation.

After many false starts, a railroad down the peninsula began to look highly probable when the San Francisco and San José Rail Road Company let initial construction contracts in October 1860. The weather interfered with the grading and the Civil War with the arrival of rails, but in 1863 there were a series of festive openings as trainloads of special guests were hauled to the successive ends of the line. By March of 1864 two passenger trains and one freight train were scheduled daily between San Jose and San Francisco, and in the first month of operation the line carried 16,000 passengers. Until 1868, when the expanded line was taken over by the Central Pacific, the San Francisco and San José Rail Road Company was proud of being locally built and locally financed.

As the century wore on, peninsula land prices made astonishing leaps. Summer homes frequently became year-round residences after the railroad made commuting feasible and fashionable. William Chapman Ralston, California's most exuberant booster, set one kind of style in his Belmont mansion. He built and entertained in lavish proportions. James Clair Flood followed Ralston's pattern but without his élan. Another style among the peninsula's wealthy new land-

Southbound San Francisco and San José passenger train crossing San Francisquito Creek, 1864

owners was set by Faxon Dean Atherton and maintained by James T. Watkins and other families. They preferred dignified understatement. Their homes were by no means small or lacking in any of the comforts, but they shunned gross luxuries.

No matter how modest the mansion, it would be unthinkable for the owners to do their own chores. Villages quickly sprang up around the railway stations or on the edges of the estates to house and supply the families of those who cooked, cleaned, gardened, and kept the stables of the estate owners. For the next few decades one of the major industries on the bayside of the peninsula was catering to the needs of San Francisco's wealthy. By the turn of the century San Mateo had a population of some 1,800 people, but most of its citizens were dependent directly or indirectly on the surrounding estates. Menlo Park, still a village, was similarly dependent, although the new university on its borders was beginning to change that. San Carlos was a railroad station and a few families, and Burlingame was no more than a railroad station and a country club. Only San Bruno and Colma were oriented toward the dairy and farming community.

How long this old-world situation might have lasted is a useless conjecture. The earthquake and fire of 1906 sent streams of refugees down the peninsula, and many of them chose to stay. Vast tracts of land were quickly divided into lots, and temporary housing was put up in San Bruno and Daly City. To their horror, the wealthy young men of the Burlingame Country Club discovered a village developing around what had been their private railroad station. San Francisco's less wealthy citizens had discovered the advantages of rural living and the apparent pleasures of commuting into the city, just like the nobs. Life on the peninsula had turned yet another corner.

42

Ralston-Sharon House

In 1853 Leonetto Cipriani, a Corsican deeply involved in Italy's military and political struggles toward unification, built a home in the peaceful isolation of Belmont. He sold it in 1864 to William Chapman Ralston, San Francisco's flamboyant financier. Over the next twelve years, Ralston expanded Cipriani's modest villa into a Victorian palace. Ralston's country place was not to be simply a pleasant home for his family, but an opulent setting in which to entertain and impress potential investors in his many business ventures as well as nearly every socially, financially, and politically important visitor to San Francisco.

After Ralston's death in 1876, the house and its numerous supporting buildings (300 people were employed to maintain the estate) were taken over by his partner, William Sharon. Sharon was less a showman than Ralston, but he continued to use the house in the grand manner for which it was designed, holding a splendid reception for Ulysses S. Grant in 1879, and another for President Rutherford B. Hayes in 1880. Sharon died in 1885, but his family occupied the house until 1889. In 1895 the building was sold. It became first a girls' finishing school and later a private sanitarium.

In 1922 the Ralston-Sharon house and some of its grounds were purchased by the Sisters of Notre Dame de Namur to serve as the campus for their college. The Sisters have done much to restore the interior of the building to its former magnificence. It is now furnished with Victorian antiques, some of which were originally the Ralstons'.

Ralston-Sharon House, 1886

The exterior of the house defies categorization. It is often described as modified Italian villa. The removal of much of its exterior decoration when the nuns had it stuccoed for easier maintenance, and the rambling nature of its growth, make even this vague term suspect. It was built of redwood, painted white before the college took it over, and rests on stone foundation pads with brick foundation walls and piers.

The interior of the house has retained much of architectural interest. The Sisters refer to the general style as "steamboat Gothic." A sun parlor on the first floor was apparently modeled after the promenade deck of a riverboat, and the open flow from room to room, managed by an inordinate number of sliding doors and curtain-window doors, is decidedly reminiscent of the great

Mezzanine, right, and dining room, below

44

Ralston-Sharon House, 1975

Mississippi boats. The mezzanine of the main stairway has an unusual design, resembling a set of opera boxes. Leaning against the silver-plated railings between the paired Ionic pillars, one overlooks the foyer lighted from above by an enormous skylight. Pierced wooden panels surround the skylight to allow warm air to escape, a device employed in many of the rooms likely to become overheated by large groups of people.

Throughout the house Ralston made extravagant use of glass, much of it cut or etched—in doors, sliding window-walls, mirrors (there are fourteen in the ballroom alone), and chandeliers. In the dining room a clock has been built into the mirror in the sideboard, and slightly smaller mirrors at each end of the wall balance and repeat the sideboard's shape. Glass-paneled doors conceal service entries and a safe for the silver. The opposite wall is the famous curtain-wall that Ralston loved to raise dramatically (into a recess between two walls on the next floor) when his guests had assembled for dinner. All of the uncovered floors are parquet, combining mahogany, walnut, cedar, and maple in a variety of patterns.

The house was declared a National Landmark in 1966, and a State Landmark in 1972.

Watkins-Cartan House

JAMES THOMAS WATKINS, a captain of the Pacific Mail Steamship Company, and his wife moved from Maryland to California in 1852. They lived in the then fashionable South Park of San Francisco. After regular train service to the peninsula was established in 1863, they and many of their friends looked for land to build country homes.

In 1866 the Watkinses bought eighteen acres on the edge of the estate of Faxon Dean Atherton, a longtime friend and one of the first of the San Franciscans to move to Menlo Park. The numerous large valley oaks on the land provided the estate with its name, Fair Oaks, and the estate provided the name for the nearby railroad stop and the lane running along one edge of the property.

During his many years at sea, Commodore Watkins developed great respect for the skill of ship carpenters, so it was to them he turned

Mrs. James T. Watkins with her son and his family on the steps of Fair Oaks, 1889

when he came to build his house. Undoubtedly the peculiar circumstances of their craft taught them to value sturdy construction, and as a result Fair Oaks withstood the trauma of being moved a number of blocks to a new site in 1903 and of a major earthquake three years later. When the Henry Cartans, the owners since 1945, were doing some renovation, they discovered one of the secrets of the house's strength in the double, criss-crossed sheathe between the inner and the outer walls.

The Watkinses chose the currently popular Gothic Revival style for their house. The design was spacious without being ostentatious, in keeping with the character of the estates around them. Steeply pitched roofs and dormers give a vertical emphasis to the house, which is further increased by the tall, narrow windows in the dormers and high front gable. Each gable has a small, round attic window at its peak. Eaves and gables are ornamented with moldings and paired brackets.

As if to soften the verticality of the house, flattened Tudor arches were used on the wide veranda, in the frame of the main entry, and in the upstairs windows. The slender porch pillars have stylized capitals. Doors and windows off the veranda and the window in the front gable are capped with drip moldings. Much of the original flint glass can still be seen in the upper windows. There is a particularly high and wide transom light just above the large double-leaved doors; this light does much to brighten the main entry hall.

The house changed hands several times after it was sold by the Watkins family in 1890. The heavily decorated ceilings in the downstairs rooms were destroyed in the 1906 earthquake and replaced with less elaborately decorated plaster. The original spiral staircase in the central hall was modified by adding a landing and a half-turn after a visiting child broke her leg sliding down the banister. Part of the veranda on the left side has been glassed in. Other additions have been very successfully incorporated in the back section. The lovely carved wood and marble mantelpieces remain untouched.

46

Watkins-Cartan House, 1975

North elevation

47

Menlo Park
Railroad Station

THE EFFECT of the San Francisco and San José Rail Road on Menlo Park was basic. It provided the name (by use of a local landmark), an economy (by bringing wealthy landowners in need of servants), and a railroad station around which to grow. The landmark was a huge triple arch with the words "Menlo Park, August 1854" carved on it. It was apparently left behind by unsuccessful squatters, but when the railroad arrived in 1863, it provided the stop with a name.

The original Menlo Park depot was probably little more than a lean-to shed, since it was easily loaded on a flatcar and moved to Belmont in 1867. It was replaced with a sturdy little three-room redwood structure, 21 x 37 feet overall. On the track side a small gable roof over the ticket window intersects with the main roof. Gable peaks were decorated with finials and carved "drops."

The ladies' waiting room on the southeast end featured a flat-roofed, polygonal window. A flat little canopy over the door was supported by fancily carved brackets. Shortly after the station opened, a small ell was added at the back for ladies' toilets. All doors and windows had drip moldings.

The interior walls of the station are tongue-and-groove redwood. The stationmaster's office in the center of the building was separated from the general waiting room on the northwest by large glass ticket windows mounted on a counter of drawers and cabinets.

Menlo Park Railroad Station, 1885

Menlo Park Railroad Station, 1975

The Menlo Park Station was a plain functional building, and by 1890 it seemed hardly grand enough for the customers it was serving. By then it was the station used by Leland Stanford, president of the Southern Pacific Railroad, which now owned the old San Francisco and San José. It also served as Stanford University's station. Renovation was clearly in order. The building was extended fifteen feet on the northwest and an ell for men's toilets was added at the back. A rectangular five-window bay was built under the trackside gable, and the roof was extended to give it a porchlike cover. The original track-side doors were converted to windows; double doors in the new addition provided access to the main waiting room.

The decorative elements added to the basic structure indulged all the fanciful taste of the time, combining Victorian Gothic, Queen Anne, and Stick-Eastlake styles. Brackets and moldings were attached to the eaves, and wooden members and panels were set out in the gables. The gable ends were covered with decorative shingles. The roof ridges received a scalloped crest, and shingled canopies were added to all windows and doors. The ladies' waiting room was treated to

lace curtains, marble-topped tables, and a black
horsehair sofa.

A waiting shed was added during World War I
to accommodate the many travelers to and from
Camp Fremont, a temporary army camp adjacent
to the station. The only alterations since the
building ceased to function as a ticket agency
have been minor. A window on the street side
was made into a door, and various accommoda-
tions for modern heat and lighting were made
in the 1960's by the current lessee, the Menlo
Park Chamber of Commerce.

Southeast elevation

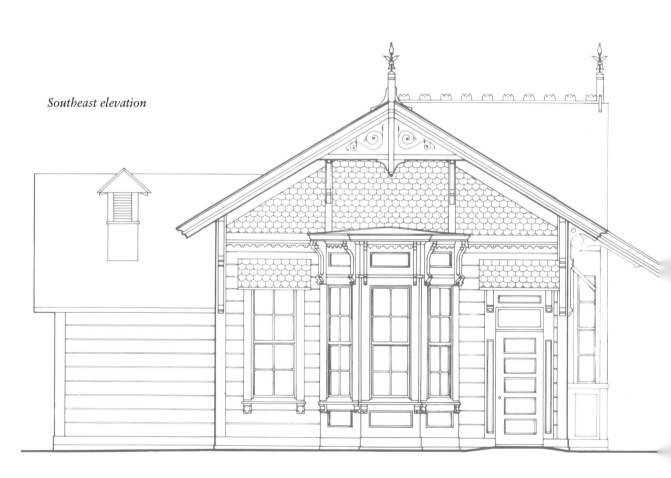

50

Church of the Nativity

THE CHURCH of the Nativity is an example of Gothic Revival architecture, which was popular throughout America well into the twentieth century, and it was the choice of the Menlo Park Catholic community when building their church in 1872. The builder, James R. Doyle, demonstrated a remarkably strict adherence to the Gothic Revival style in detail as well as form. The addition in 1887 of the transept nave and chancel was accomplished with scrupulous fidelity to the original idiom.

For many years the only Catholic place of worship between San Francisco and Santa Clara was the little schoolhouse-church built in the 1850's

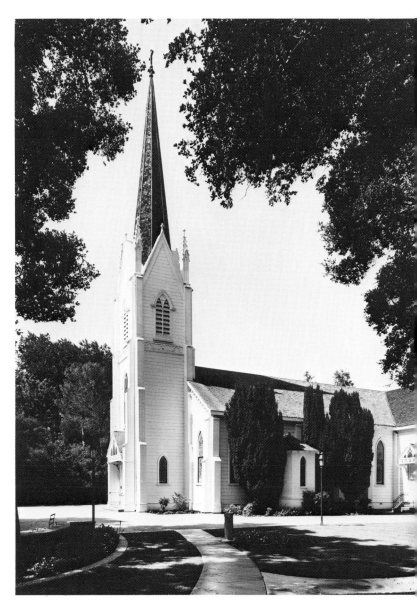

Main entrance

by Dennis Martin and abandoned in 1876 when he lost title to his land. As the forests were denuded of their timber and the source of employment for many Irish Catholics shifted to the flat bayside, Catholic churches were built in Redwood City (1862), San Mateo (1863), and Mayfield (1869). When easy railroad transportation encouraged many wealthy Catholic families to establish country homes in the Menlo Park area,

51

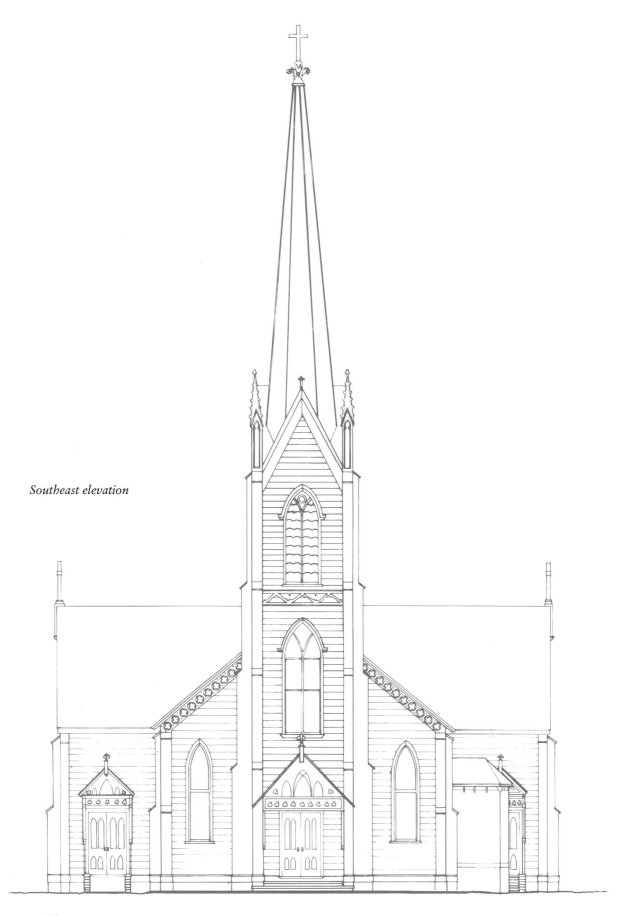

Southeast elevation

52

Rear view showing rose window

The church is 62 x 137 feet with a 120-foot spire. The characteristic Gothic Revival detailing is evident in the paired lancet windows with drip moldings in the main tower. Single lancet windows are used elsewhere. The tower is decorated with finials and crockets. Simple quatrefoil tracery decorates the eaves of the façade and the gable. The canopy over the main door is paneled and braced with lancet and trefoil designs. The lancet motif is repeated dramatically in the interior with exposed redwood hammerbeam trusses.

Undoubtedly the church's design was dictated by the tastes of the time, for it is clearly in harmony with the surviving houses of that day. Fair Oaks is a good example. But there is ample evidence that the purity of its style still has great appeal to the parishioners. When population pressure in the 1950's prompted talk of replacing the church with a larger, modern structure, local churchgoers were adamantly opposed. The strength of their conviction can be seen in the care given the building and its grounds.

the construction of another Catholic church seemed appropriate.

St. Bridget's, as the Menlo Park church was first called, was originally built on a lot donated by Robert E. Doyle, but when Doyle's land became entangled in legal difficulties, the lot was sold and the church purchased its present three-acre site on Oak Grove Avenue. For some reason the church was not moved directly to the new site but was first moved across the railroad tracks to Santa Cruz Avenue for a few months. This series of moves prompted local wags to dub it The Roaming Catholic Church.

In 1887 a brick foundation was inserted and the new transept nave and chancel were added, producing the present Latin Cross plan. At the consecration of the completed church in 1888, it was given its present name, Church of the Nativity. Very few alterations have been made since then, although the rose window over the altar was donated in 1900. The 1906 earthquake did little damage to the church, but the rectory next door was destroyed.

Interior view toward altar

Linden Towers

JAMES CLAIR FLOOD came to California in 1849, panned some gold, lost it in the 1855 panic, and with a partner opened a depression-safe business, a saloon. With a location next to the Mining Exchange in San Francisco, Flood and his partner, William S. O'Brien, soon turned the conversations they overheard into a fortune, and after gaining control over the Comstock mines they manipulated the fortune into several more. In his heyday Flood was reputed to be the wealthiest man in California.

Like all the other wealthy men, Flood first built a mansion in San Francisco and then looked around for a site for a country home. He found it in Menlo Park—300 acres of flat, parklike land to which he later added 2,400 acres of adjoining marshland. He commissioned Augustus J. Laver and later William Curlett to build him a house finer than any in the West. Construction began on his white palace in 1878, after several cottages were built in Menlo Park to house the carpenters.

Linden Towers was three stories high and topped by a 150-foot tower and a few lesser towers. Although made of wood, it was often compared to marble by admirers, or wedding cake by detractors. The house was said to have 40 or more rooms, and some of the closets were so large that the count occasionally rose as high as 100.

Interior walls were finished with richly carved hardwood paneling, with one room entirely in Indian teak, another in rosewood, and so on. A sample of every known kind of wood was claimed to have been used somewhere in the

Linden Towers, 1881

54

Entrance to Linden Towers

and barrel—to the University of California. Even though she included an endowment toward its upkeep, the University concluded in 1903 that the estate was going to be too costly to maintain and deeded it back to her. In 1904 her brother, James L. Flood, decided to live in it. He added an elegant garage and mechanics' shop for his collection of motorcars, and built two handsome metal gates and the mile-long brick wall that still identifies the Linden Towers frontage.

In 1934 James's widow declared the house a relic from another era and announced she would auction off the furniture and have the house and its outbuildings razed. In 1936 the house was torn down, and the land was gradually subdivided. All that remain now of the Floods' palace are a few pieces of garden statuary, their son's symbolic fence, and, of course, the legend of Linden Towers' opulence.

house. Mantelpieces were of marble, and stained-glass windows were abundant. Frescoes painted by famous Italian artists covered many ceilings. The bathrooms had silver fixtures and enormous marble tubs.

The furnishing of Linden Towers was supervised by New York decorators, Pottier and Stylmer, and the results were as luxurious as the house, including such items as a $7,000 bed of Santo Domingo mahogany and $100-a-yard velvet and brocade hangings. The billiard table was hand-carved, and the cues were inlaid with mother-of-pearl.

Surrounding the great white mansion were twenty-two acres of lawns and flowerbeds studded with statuary, fountains, marble steps, and balustrades. The stable was as palatial as the house. The exterior design was similar, and each stall was styled in a different specimen of rare wood.

All this grandeur surrounding a man who rose from very humble beginnings brought raised eyebrows from many who had themselves struck it rich only a few decades earlier. Perhaps this is why Flood's daughter, who inherited the estate after her mother's death, donated it—lock, stock,

55

Burlingame Railroad Station

MANY BUILDINGS in California trace their architectural inspiration to this well-designed railroad station. Mission Revival became a very popular style at the turn of the century, and all the elements associated with it were used here.

In 1893 a group of San Francisco's wealthiest young men organized the Burlingame Country Club, California's first. The railway stop nearest their club had a simple shelter which the members considered inadequate to their needs. Negotiations with Southern Pacific produced an agreement that would give the club freedom to design and build the station, with the railroad contributing the cost of an ordinary depot.

A. Page Brown, a member of the club, focused national attention on the Mission Revival style in his design for the California building at the Columbian Exposition in Chicago in 1893. Although the Burlingame Station was designed by fellow members George H. Howard, Jr. and J. B. Mathison, they used many elements of Brown's exposition designs: the rough stucco imitation of adobe, tile roofs, long arcades, and pseudo-Moorish detailing.

Burlingame Railroad Station, 1899

The station was divided into three sections: the baggage room on the northwest end, the waiting room in the center, and living quarters for the stationmaster on the southeast end. Roof tiles for all three sections were handmade by mission Indians. Those used on the main roof were salvaged from an old shelter built about 1793 as an outpost of Mission Dolores in San Francisco. Those on the residential section came from the decaying remnants of Mission San Antonio de Padua, near Jolon.

Distinguished features of a number of California missions were incorporated, such as Mission Carmel's lovely quatrefoil window in the scalloped gable of the trackside façade, but the design was not dependent on any particular mission. The tile roofs are given importance by wide overhangs, and the graceful round arches and broad arcades typical of Mission Revival are well rendered. The square central tower has a low hipped roof. There are projecting beams on the exterior and exposed beams as a decorative element in the waiting room. The design included a terraced roof, but stairs were never built to reach it. The missions did not have fireplaces, so the chimneys on the station were a much copied solution to an architectural problem of adaptation.

Innovative construction techniques were used, such as balloon framing. The building was sheathed with diagonal redwood siding, tar paper, and chicken wire coated with heavy, rough pebble stucco simulating plastered adobe.

For more than a decade the station stood in an open field at the foot of a long lane bordered by eucalyptus and cypress trees. The 1906 earthquake did no damage to the station, but destroyed its isolation. Many families who chose to rebuild outside San Francisco were attracted by a Burlingame address. The village that grew around the station was not at all to the liking of the members of the Burlingame Country Club. They responded by incorporating the town of Hillsborough in an attempt to preserve the rural quality of their surroundings by establishing minimum lot-size requirements and other building restrictions.

Burlingame Railroad Station, 1975

Street side

Bank of San Mateo County

THE BANK of San Mateo County, the first commercial bank on the peninsula, was incorporated in July 1891. For its first nine years it was housed in the Capitol Hotel in Redwood City, but in 1899 the bank purchased the northwest corner of Main and Broadway and announced that it would build the county's first stone building. This feat had been accomplished in 1865 by the Church of St. Matthew, but the bank did build the county's first stone veneer structure.

Alfred I. Coffey of San Francisco designed for the bank a Renaissance Revival brick building faced with stone from Utah. The flat-roofed, two-story structure has sheet-metal pediments, cornices, and dome. Neoclassical detailing is evident in the use of colossal-order composite pilasters and projecting pediments with cornice blocks. The corner treatment is a form popular to the

Carved stone eagle

Bank of San Mateo County, April 1906. The Pioneer Store is behind the fallen dome.

area and time, but more commonly expressed in wood. A semicircular colonnaded entrance porch supports a bay window and is capped by a high ribbed dome and a flagpole.

When this modern and substantial building opened its doors in 1900, the tellers' cages had not arrived and the vault was not yet complete, but a counter was improvised by laying a plank across two barrel heads, and the bank's daily receipts were deposited in the county's safe, which was in the back of the Pioneer Store (see page 11). P. P. Chamberlain, owner of the Pioneer Store and county treasurer, was also a vice-president of the bank.

The 1906 earthquake shook the Broadway front of the bank into the street and dumped the dome and its flagpole into the center of the intersection. The damage looked serious, but in fact

58

Bank of San Mateo County with Fitzpatrick Building on the left

the basic structure was unharmed. Within two months the building was again serving customers.

As a result of the organization in 1904 of the San Mateo County Savings Bank under the same management, the Bank of San Mateo County needed more space. The bank's directors bought the Ross Building next door and commissioned Coffey to integrate the additional 55-foot front-age on Broadway. He was remarkably successful, for the two buildings now appear to be one. In the closed-up former entrance to the bank building's upper floor, a carved stone eagle was installed with the date of completion, 1910 A.D.

For thirty years the building of the Bank of San Mateo County stood as a proud and slightly pugnacious symbol of the city's progress, but in

59

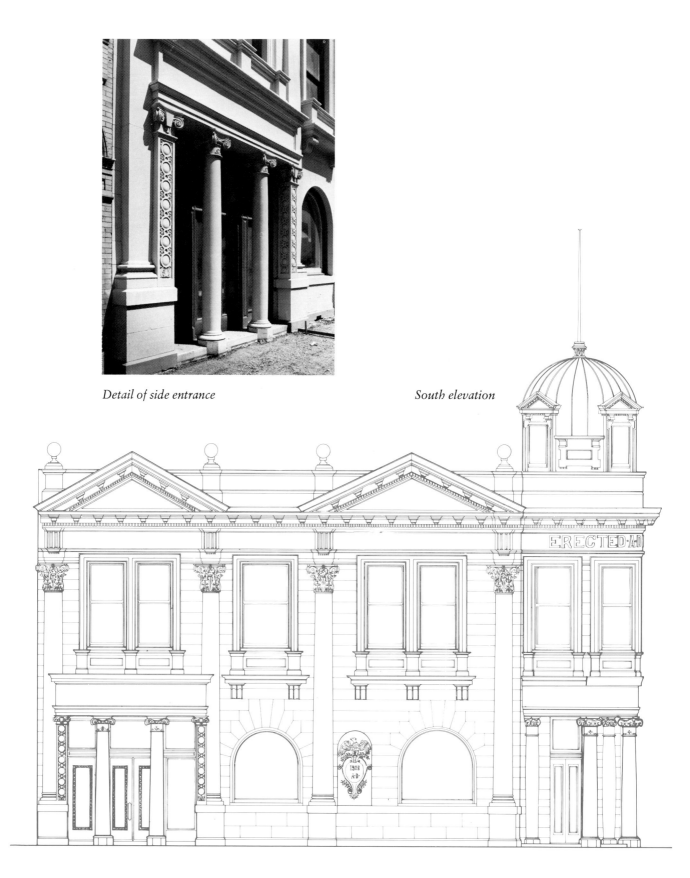

Detail of side entrance   *South elevation*

60

1930 the savings bank moved out, and in 1941 the First National Bank, as the original bank was then known, moved into a new but nondescript building across the street. Louis Behrens, the son of a founder of the bank, and his wife purchased the old building for sentimental reasons. During World War II it was occupied by the Office of Price Administration, and in 1963 a finance corporation rented it, refurbished it, and went bankrupt before its opening.

In 1971 the building was sold, with the stipulation that the façade be preserved, to a promoter who wanted to combine the bank, the neighboring Fitzpatrick Building, and the Pioneer Store into a business complex to be called the Redwood City Industrial Mart. Work was well under way when a misunderstanding arose between the developer and the city about demolition of a condemned wooden building at the back of the bank. Attempts to meet the city's stringent building codes eventually bankrupted the developer, and another opportunity to rejuvenate the old bank was lost.

Fitzpatrick Building

THE TWO-STORY brick building adjoining the Bank of San Mateo County was built in 1905 by the same architect and the same builder. Although the terra cotta brick façade is quite different in style, it is compatible with its elegant neighbor. The Palladian windows and heavily bracketed cornice give the building dignity without undue heaviness. The upper floor housed the law practice of the owner, Edward F. Fitzpatrick, and after his death that of his son, Joseph R. Fitzpatrick. The building now stands vacant, apparently because potential buyers find bringing it up to building code standards prohibitively expensive.

Fitzpatrick Building

San Mateo County Courthouse

IF SAN MATEO County does not hold a record
for the number of its county courthouses—
four in its 120-year history—it surely must have
the record for the number severely damaged by
earthquakes, two out of the four. The fourth,
whose stately dome continues to dominate the
landscape about it in Redwood City, had been
accepted by the Board of Supervisors but not
yet occupied when the 1906 earthquake struck.

The courthouse was designed by George A.
Dodge and J. W. Dolliver in 1903. It is a rare
Bay Area example of civic architecture in the

San Mateo County Courthouse, ca. 1912

San Mateo County Courthouses, April 1906

62

San Mateo County Courthouse, 1975

Roman-Renaissance style. The exterior of the building, faced with warm-toned Colusa sandstone, achieves power and reserved grandeur through such elements as colossal-order pilasters with American eagle capitals, and a massive balustrade and parapet. Eagles, carved in stone, perch on the tips of the parapets.

The 116-foot dome and its massive panels of stained glass came through the earthquake un-harmed. During reconstruction it was discovered that the dome was the secondary cause of much of the damage to the rest of the building. Its steel cage had never been bolted to the foundation, and in the rocking of the earth its great weight exerted the influence of an inverted pendulum on the structure around it. It is now supported by lattice riveted steel with direct and independent supports to the ground.

Second floor of rotunda. Dome at right.

dor of the dome, are sixteen arched stained-glass windows. The eight ornate ribs between the dome's panels of stained glass are firmly attached to the rotunda by wreathed eagles on a shield of stars and stripes.

This second edition of the fourth San Mateo County Courthouse was estimated to cost the taxpayers $175,000, and in the end it cost $500,000. The revised design was drawn by Glenn Allen in 1907. Reconstruction took three years, marked by delays, plan changes, overpayments, and scandal. Finally, on June 23, 1910, the Board of Supervisors met for the first time in the new courthouse.

In 1933 the need for more space was solved by adding a three-story Federal-style addition. A less appropriate style could hardly be imagined. The addition also necessitated the removal of the elegant main entrance with its massive Corinthian columns. A second, smaller annex was added on the opposite side in 1941.

The richness of the building is now in its interior. Light plays through the stained glass over the central rotunda onto handsome mosaic floors. A grand stairway leads to the balcony-like second floor and its finely drafted iron balustrades. Imitation green marble (scagliola) columns topped by elaborately carved capitals line the walls. Above them, building up to the splen-

64

Chapter Four

Leland Stanford's Farm
1870's-1900's

THE MIDPENINSULA developed slowly up to the 1880's. The village of Menlo Park lived off the estates of a few wealthy landowners, and Mayfield, now part of Palo Alto, supplied the farmers of the area. When Governor and Mrs. Leland Stanford announced in 1885 that they would turn their Palo Alto Stock Farm into a university, the pattern of development on the peninsula began to change. The building of the university brought in a whole new population of stonecutters, draftsmen, masons, gardeners, car-penters, teamsters, and laborers. Their families came with them, and the bakers, butchers, and blacksmiths soon followed. By 1906 the uni-versity's town, Palo Alto, was one of the more important towns on the peninsula.

After their marriage in Albany in 1850, Leland and Jane Stanford made their first home together in the raw Wisconsin town of Port Washington, where Leland had established his first law practice two years earlier. In 1852 Leland's law office and large collection of law books were de-

Stanford University, ca. 1902

consolate and resentful Jane behind to care for her ailing father.

Following his brothers' lead, but not joining them, Stanford at once opened a general store in a small mining camp in Eldorado County called Cold Springs. When trade there began to fall off, he sold out and opened up in a more promising Placer County town called Michigan City (later known as Michigan Bluff). By May 1855 when Stanford received word of his father-in-law's death, Michigan City had grown from a camp of 30 people to a town of 2,000, and Stanford had received comparable returns on his investment. He sold out at once and returned to New York State, planning to go into the same business there. His wife, fuming with humiliation over the gossips' explanation of her long sojourn in Albany, urged him to return to California, taking her with him. They set off together later that year on a venture that would take them on paths neither could have imagined.

Back in Sacramento, Stanford bought the large general store owned by his two brothers Josiah and Philip and began to develop other business interests. In 1861 he and three other Sacramento merchants, Charles Crocker, Mark Hopkins, and Collis P. Huntington, became interested in Theodore Judah's scheme to build a railroad across the continent. In June of that year the four businessmen took out formal incorporation papers, and the Central Pacific Railroad, soon to be the most powerful organization in the West, was under way. It would bring all four fantastic wealth. Stanford also became active in the fledgling Republican Party. He ran unsuccessfully for various state offices before he was elected to a single but pivotal term as Civil War governor in 1862.

In 1868, after eighteen years of marriage, the Stanfords' only child, Leland Jr., was born. The following year Stanford, as president of the Central Pacific, traveled to Utah to drive in the symbolic golden spike that joined the Eastern and Western parts of the nation's first transcontinental railroad. The family moved to San Francisco in 1874, and two years later Stanford bought Mayfield Grange, a beautiful farm on the banks

stroyed by fire. Faced with a steadily dwindling law practice resulting from economic changes in the area, Leland sold his various bits of property, and the discouraged couple returned to Albany. Five of Leland's brothers had gone to California, and his family urged him to join them. Jane was apparently in favor of the move, but her father would not hear of it. In June 1852 Leland sailed alone for California, leaving a dis-

of San Francisquito Creek, the boundary of San Mateo and Santa Clara counties. Beginning with this property he gradually acquired more than 8,800 acres of land, making his estate the largest on the peninsula. Here he pursued his interests in agriculture and the breeding and training of racehorses. As their son grew older, the Stanfords spent more and more of their time at the farm, where the boy was happiest.

In May 1883 the Stanford family set off on a leisurely tour of Europe to enjoy their last months together before young Leland entered Harvard University in September 1884. In Athens in mid-January, Leland Jr. complained of a sore throat and headache. In Naples he was again unwell, and in Rome his condition grew worse. In Florence in the middle of March 1884, Leland Jr. died of typhoid fever. He was not yet sixteen years old.

Desolated by his death, his parents vowed to leave the vast fortune that would have been his to all the young people of California in the form of a university built on the farm where Leland had been happy. Within two months of their loss they were interviewing presidents of Eastern universities in search of a sharper definition of their goals.

The Founding Grant of Stanford University, executed on November 11, 1885, defined the university's scope, purpose, and organization. It called for the tuition-free admission of men and women on equal terms, and established a Board of Trustees with no duties so long as either Stanford lived. Stanford died in 1893, Mrs. Stanford in 1905. After her death, their entire estate, valued at more than $30 million, became the inalienable property of the university. At the time this amount was greater than any other American university's endowment.

Rancho Matadero

DAVID STARR JORDAN, Stanford's first president, was a scientist of international reputation whose books *The Genera of Fishes* (1917-20) and *A Classification of Fishes* (1923) are still considered authoritative. He was also a gifted storyteller, and his tales (most of them pure fabrications) about a mysterious Frenchman named Peter Coutts, who in the 1870's owned and farmed a good part of what is now the Stanford campus, have been widely accepted as true. What now seems reasonably clear is that Jean-Baptiste-Paulin Caperon, a wealthy Frenchman whose liberal political opinions resulted in his exile, traveled to San Francisco in 1874 on the Swiss passport of his deceased cousin, Viscount Peter Coutts, bought a house on California Street, and sent for his wife and children and their governess. In 1875 he bought 1,400 acres adjacent to Mayfield Grange. Caperon named his estate after the creek that formed one of its boundaries. He

imported California's first Holstein-Friesian cattle from Holland and established the finest Ayreshire herds in the state.

In 1882, while on a visit abroad, Caperon sold the ranch and all its livestock and furnishings to his neighbor Leland Stanford, who christened it the Running Ranch to distinguish it from his own Trotting Ranch. The house was closed, not to be opened again until 1887.

Escondité

The cottage Caperon built for his family in 1875 on what is now Escondido Road was intended as a temporary residence to be used until the brick mansion he envisioned on a nearby knoll could be built. He had the knoll thickly planted with Monterey pines in preparation for landscaping around his future home. The area is now a faculty housing district on the Stanford campus known as Pine Hill 1.

Caperon's board-and-batten cottage combines Victorian Gothic and Italianate styles. Originally the gable ridge was a lacy wooden crest. The

Escondité, ca. 1892

Escondité, 1975

eaves are unusually wide, and in the gable ends there are modified stick decorations. The tall windows have heavy drip moldings with modified consoles at the corners. There are polygonal bay windows on both ends of the main wing. The exterior foundation walls are wood scored to resemble stone.

If Caperon had a name for his cottage, it was not remembered. David Starr Jordan and his family lived there in their first years at Stanford, and it was Jordan who gave it the name Escondité, a French version of the Spanish *escondido* (hidden). Prior to the Jordans' arrival in 1891, the cottage was occupied by Charles Allerton Coolidge, the architect working on plans for the university. The young man seemed content with his quarters, but the new president's wife found the cottage deplorably lacking in modern plumbing. The first entrance exams to the university were administered on the veranda of Escondité.

After the Jordans moved into their own home in 1894, Escondité was closed again except for a brief period when it housed athletes in training. After John McGilvray accepted the contract to build the Outer Quad in 1898, he and his family moved into the cottage and stayed for nineteen years. During their occupancy the original shutters were removed, the veranda screened, and two bathrooms added. The next longest residents were Professor Eliot Blackwelder and his family (1922-49), who greatly changed the appearance of the house by adding a second story and a large sleeping porch. The building is now used for university offices.

Frenchman's Library

Caperon collected rare books and documents. As soon as he had completed the construction of his cottage and the essential barns, he had his workmen build a separate library building for his collection. The weight of the books required a substantial structure, and the fact that some of them were extremely valuable made brick the logical fire-resistant choice.

The building has a very low-pitched roof with extremely wide eaves. Above the main cornice and at the ends and edges of the veranda roofs there is a latticework trim that was formerly repeated as a balustrade on the veranda. The brick walls are unusually thick. The outstanding architectural feature of the house was

Frenchman's Library, before 1900

Frenchman's Library, 1975

its three-story tower topped by a four-sided Norman steeple with three narrow Gothic dormer windows on each side, each smaller than the one below it. The windows had metal finials at the top, and the peak of the steeple sported an elaborate weather vane. The steeple was later replaced by a square, many-windowed room. A wooden bay window was also added to the front of the library, and the structure was painted yellow.

The Stanfords first used the library as an office for the Running Ranch and a night school for Stanford farm employees. In 1891 it was briefly the first administrative office for the new university. Prior to 1960 it served as faculty housing, and it has since housed a variety of university projects.

Frenchman's Tower

On the west bank of Matadero Creek, just before it reaches the bay plains, there is a 50-foot brick tower that looks more like the remains of an Irish watchtower than anything one might expect in the California countryside. The crenelated top and lancet windows (now bricked in) add to the fairy-tale effect. The tower is empty and is too porous to have ever held water. For years passersby have puzzled over the reason for its construction, but it apparently had no other function than to mark the extreme southeast corner of Caperon's estate—and perhaps to keep his workmen busy in the off season.

Frenchman's Tower, before 1900

Frenchman's Tower, 1975

72

Palo Alto Winery

LELAND STANFORD'S interest in wine production began in 1868, when he purchased the Warm Springs Ranch near San José. The existing winery on that ranch was enlarged, and Stanford's brother took over its management. When Stanford bought the Palo Alto Stock Farm in 1876, he planted acres of high-quality wine grapes. In the 1880's Stanford also purchased the 55,000-acre Vina Ranch in northern California's Tehema County, where he produced a good-quality grape brandy.

Until 1886, when Stanford gave his brother title to the Warm Springs Ranch, all the grapes from the Palo Alto farm were hauled to Warm Springs for pressing. Construction of a winery on the Palo Alto Stock Farm was finished in 1888, and from then on wine was produced there and sold under the Palo Alto label.

Stanford saw no conflict between his winery and his university. Indeed, he held that wine drinking in moderation was likely to discourage the immoderate use of stronger liquor. Appalled by the thriving saloons to the west and east of the campus, the Stanfords banned the sale of liquor by restrictive covenants in the land deeds to University Park (now northern Palo Alto), a tract to the northeast acquired by the Stanfords in 1887. In 1894, the year after her husband's death, Mrs. Stanford ordered John F. Lewis, the manager of the Palo Alto Winery, to sell wine in case lots only and to see to it that the cases were shipped out. Lewis had been amiably dispensing wine to students who brought their own containers.

The winery was closed in 1915, when the momentum toward Prohibition made the ratification of the Eighteenth Amendment inevitable. The vineyards were uprooted and the land planted to hay or leased to truck farmers for tomatoes and strawberries. There was talk of converting the winery into a dormitory, but instead it and 250 acres of the farm were leased to the Carnation Milk Company for a dairy. From then until 1958 the old winery was used by one company or another as a cattle barn. The American Breeders Association moved their prize bulls to Wisconsin in 1958 following the construction of a new hospital to the south and a new shopping center to the north.

For a brief period the winery stood vacant while planners sought ways to return it to productive use. Finally in 1961 John S. Bolles, a San Francisco architect, and a group of investors remodeled the winery into two floors of shops and offices, with a bank and a restaurant complex.

Palo Alto Winery. Top, leased to the American Breeders Association, 1950's. Bottom, now the Old Stanford Barn.

73

Leland Stanford Junior University

In 1885 General Francis A. Walker, president of Massachusetts Institute of Technology and one of the men the Stanfords consulted on their sad homeward journey in 1884, urged them to entrust the general design of their university to Frederick Law Olmsted, the landscape architect who created Central Park in New York City. In 1886 Olmsted, Walker, and Stanford met together on the farm and considered various sites. Olmsted preferred the foothills for their view of the bay and because they were an ideal setting for the kind of naturalistic design he liked. Stanford disagreed. He insisted on a level site as being more suitable for the formal, symmetrical design he wanted and as offering more possibilities for expansion.

Olmsted's "preliminary plan," which was considerably influenced by Stanford, established the general concept of long, low buildings unified by arcades into quadrangles. The plan was developed into drawings for specific buildings by Charles Allerton Coolidge, the junior partner of Shepley, Rutan & Coolidge, a Boston architectural firm. The firm had recently been reorganized after the death of its distinguished founder, Henry Hobson Richardson, whose influence on his younger colleagues was pronounced.

The earliest Coolidge drawings have been lost, but an impressionistic sketch made by a San Francisco newsman in 1887 indicates that they were quite different from the drawings presented at the laying of the cornerstone. Rather than making the church the main focus of a stiffly symmetrical plan, Coolidge had the main entrance to the campus frame a long view of the hills and trees to the south. Coolidge wrote unhappily to Olmsted in early May complaining that the Stanfords were insisting on an enormous memorial arch at the entry, and were in general determined to be rid of "the very quietness and reserve which we like so much in it."

Stanford said repeatedly that the university should have "an architecture distinctly Californian in character," for which he looked to the California missions built under the direction of Franciscan priests in the eighteenth and early nineteenth centuries. The dilapidated condition of the missions by the 1850's left Stan-

The north side of the Inner Quad, 1891

The north side of the Outer Quad, 1905

The Coolidge drawing of the campus

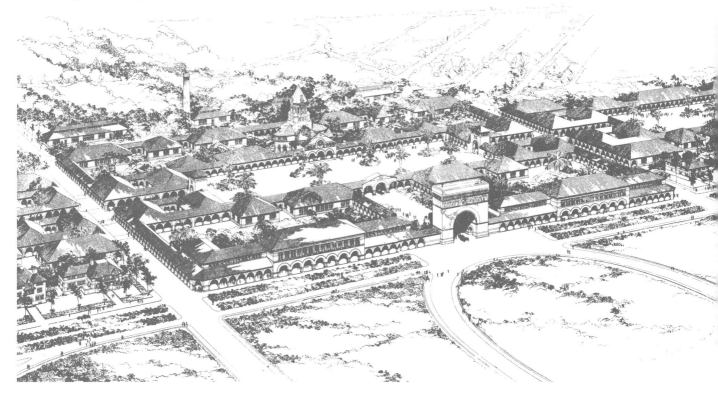

in fact derived from Romanesque, it lacked the monumental qualities the Stanfords sought. Not so Richardson's version of Romanesque, which was exactly what Leland Stanford wanted.

The changes the Stanfords desired were hurriedly incorporated into Coolidge's drawings in time for the laying of the cornerstone on May 14, 1887, the anniversary of young Leland's birth. The revised plans showed a fiercely symmetrical design of quadrangles and an oversized Memorial Arch at the entrance to the campus, leading toward a grandiose Memorial Church. The Inner Quad consisted of twelve one-story buildings on an east-west axis connected by a continuous open arcade surrounding a three-acre courtyard. Within the courtyard there were eight circular beds to be planted with semitropical trees and shrubs.

Memorial Arch from Memorial Court, 1905

ford free to imagine their original state, and two of the elements he particularly favored—red tile roofs and the use of unbroken arcades connecting and unifying the buildings around courtyards—became prominent features of the university's architecture. Significantly, both tile roofs and Roman arches were characteristic of the Romanesque of southern France and Spain, a style greatly favored by Coolidge's mentor Richardson. Though California mission architecture was

Arcade, Inner Quad

History Corner

commonness. They appeared to me exactly like a factory." Faculty wives arrived to find inadequate housing, no servants, and the many other problems that beset any new community. One way or another the problems were dealt with, and opening ceremonies were held in the Inner Quad on October 1, 1891.

Less than two years later the Inner Quad was the scene of a more somber ceremony. Leland Stanford died on June 21, 1893. At his death the remainder of his estate, appraised at $17 million, was to go to his wife, but quite unexpectedly the federal government filed a claim against the estate for $15 million in partial repayment of huge government sums loaned to Stanford's Central Pacific Railroad. The money was not yet due to be repaid, and no claims had been filed against the estates of two deceased partners,

Geology Corner

Coolidge superintended the construction of the Inner Quad, the Engineering Buildings, and Encina Hall, using day labor rather than contractors to keep costs down. Several quarries were opened on the Stanford land, but more satisfactory stone was found at New Almaden, ten miles south of San Jose. A quarry of even-textured buff sandstone there was leased for $100,000, and massive rough-cut blocks were shipped to the campus by rail, where a small army of stonecutters fashioned some into broken-face ashlars and carved others with intricate decorations.

After several postponements it was decided that the university would be ready for students in the fall of 1891. To everyone's surprise, over 400 students enrolled the first year. Not all of the arriving faculty and students found the university as pleasing as its creators did. The wife of the first Registrar wrote, "What I saw, some distance off across a dry, dun waste, was a low, bare line of buildings, plain and stiff, unrelieved by greenery, lying against hills of the same dusty hue, not an arcade or a court or the least mitigation of their

78

Memorial Church

but Stanford's political enemies persisted, pressing the suit all the way to the United States Supreme Court.

For three years the university and its employees subsisted on the drastically reduced funds Mrs. Stanford was allowed by the court for "personal" expenses. Finally, facing a long wait on the Supreme Court calendar, Mrs. Stanford appealed to President Cleveland, who arranged for an early hearing. In March 1896 the Supreme Court unanimously agreed that the claim had no legal basis. It took two more years for the estate to clear probate, and another year passed before Mrs. Stanford sold the family's railroad holdings and turned the $11 million over to the University Trustees.

Jordan had managed for six lean years to maintain morale and remarkably high academic standards among his faculty. He now sought to fulfill some of his promises with increased salaries, a full slate of new appointments, and new academic programs. Mrs. Stanford, however, chose instead to move ahead with the building program, and the university entered what Jordan drily referred to as the Great Stone Age.

Beginning in 1898, Charles E. Hodges, who had been Clerk of the Works during the construction of the Inner Quad, coordinated the construction of the Outer Quad according to the Coolidge plans. John McGilvray was the contractor for all of the buildings, but detailed plans for each building were drawn by local architects. The fourteen new buildings, two and two-and-a-half stories high, were designed with their arcades on the outside, thus giving a more pleasing appearance than the outer walls of the Inner Quad. Across the north front the towering Memorial

Memorial Church, rear view

Arch gave access to Memorial Court, and it in turn opened onto the Inner Quad and the Memorial Church.

To design the frieze for the Memorial Arch the Stanfords first approached a leading American sculptor, Augustus St. Gaudens. When he proved unavailable, they turned to John Evans of Coolidge's Boston firm. The theme was the March of Civilization. The Stanfords described in detail what events they wished to appear, and Evans drew a design for local stonecarvers to execute. The decidedly unconventional result downgraded Yankee influence on California's "civilization" in favor of Spanish-Mexican influence, though it culminated in the building of the railroad. The arch itself was copied from Richardson's unexecuted design for a Civil War memorial in Buffalo.

80

After her husband's death Mrs. Stanford decided that the church should be built as a memorial to him. Ground was broken in May 1899. San Francisco architect Clinton Day used a preliminary Coolidge sketch (modeled on at least two Richardson plans) as the basis for the church design. The enormous mosaic on the façade depicting the Sermon on the Mount, the 80-foot spire housing the clock and chimes, and the huge, stained-glass rose window established the church as the focal point of the Inner Quad.

The interior of the church was equally breath-taking. Under Mrs. Stanford's direction, mosaics were made by Salviati Studios in Venice from medieval paintings of redemption scenes in the Old Testament. A notable series of mosaics in the apse represents the New Testament's fulfillment of the Old. For another mosaic

Interior, Memorial Church

Mrs. Stanford obtained papal permission to copy the Roselli fresco of the Last Supper in the Sistine Chapel. Frederick S. Lamb's nineteen stained-glass windows depicting scenes from the life of Christ were taken from modern paintings and his clerestory windows are portraits of New Testament figures and saints. The resurrection window is an original design.

During the Great Stone Age, Mrs. Stanford ordered a number of economies in building. In April 1906, a year after Mrs. Stanford's death, one of her economies became a tragedy. In the earthquake the buildings she had ordered built without steel reinforcement collapsed into heaps of rubble. The Memorial Arch and the tower of the church were destroyed, and only the Inner Quad suffered little damage. After seven years of continuous construction, Jordan declared, "We have just about what we started with."

Reconstruction started almost immediately, and soon most structures were restored. Since 1950 most of the interiors of the Quad buildings have been renovated and modernized without modifying the original exteriors.

Campus Houses

According to Olmsted's original plan, wide tree-lined streets would one day radiate out from the central campus, and on these streets would be rows of faculty houses. When the first faculty families arrived in the summer of 1891, they found nothing but empty fields. Since suitable housing in the nearby towns was extremely scarce, the university hurriedly built ten "pattern book" houses, two to a design. Students immediately dubbed the houses the Decalogue; Jordan referred to them as the Alvarado Avenue houses; and the common reference soon became "the Row."

Griffin-Drell House

The need for housing was so acute that at first six of the Row houses were shared by two families. Within a few months two larger houses were added at each end of the Row, and soon

Griffin-Drell House, 1975

Griffin-Drell House, 1892

more were built on an adjoining street. Of the original Row houses only one survives: the Griffin-Drell House, a rigidly symmetrical Queen Anne style with twin conical-roofed turrets. A duplicate of the house, built at about the same time and taken from the same pattern book, has also survived on Salvatierra Street.

John Casper Branner, who became the university's second president, lived with his family at the far end of the Row. Mrs. Branner described the houses as needing only "the line of clothes flapping in the wind to complete the picture of a poor quarter in the outskirts of some western town." Other residents were less critical, some of them enjoying for the first time the comforts of modern plumbing. Each house had a number of bedrooms on the second floor and in the garret, but only one bathroom. Heating was provided by fireplaces in the main rooms.

Dunn-Bacon House

On at least two occasions after Mr. Stanford's death, Mrs. Stanford allowed friends not associated with the university to build homes on the campus. One huge three-story summer home with a carriage house was built in 1899 by George B. Cooksey on San Juan Hill; both buildings are now fraternity houses. Another non-faculty home, the Dunn-Bacon House, was built the same year by Orrin and Harriet Dunn and today is the residence of their nephew, a professor of mathematics.

The Dunns commissioned Charles Edward Hodges, then the university's resident architect, to design a house with a traditional Greek Revival façade like those Mrs. Dunn recalled from her native Boston. The front of the house is dominated by a two-story portico supported by enormous Ionic columns and capitals. Although the house is now surrounded by academic and fraternity buildings, the rose-lined circular drive leading up to this impressive entry creates a little island of serenity.

The entry hall is a large, bright room that leads through wide doorways into adjoining rooms and gives access to the stair hall at the left. The living room, divided into two sections by columns and a balustrade, occupies the right side of the first floor. On the left is a study and a dining room. Redwood paneling and moldings have been left unpainted and now have a soft, warm quality. A discreet stairway that disappears behind a sliding panel in the parlor made it possible for the lady of the house to escape unseen from unexpected guests.

South and east sides

Durand-Kirkman House

In 1904 the Durand-Kirkman House was the first campus house to be built outside the established three-block residential area. When William F. Durand came to Stanford in 1904 to head its Department of Mechanical Engineering, he and his wife chose to build on San Juan Hill rather than in the section of Palo Alto known as Professorville. The site they chose had its drawbacks. Electricity and telephone service were not supplied for two years after the house was completed, and it was not clear how the surrounding space would be used. The house and its veranda were sited to overlook a projected street along the western edge of the Durands' lot; but when Santa Ynez Street was finally put in, it was one lot farther west.

The Durands' architect, Professor A. B. Clark of Stanford's Art Department, designed the house in the currently popular Shingle style, which was also appropriate to their site. The

Newel post and banister

West elevation.
From the original blueprint

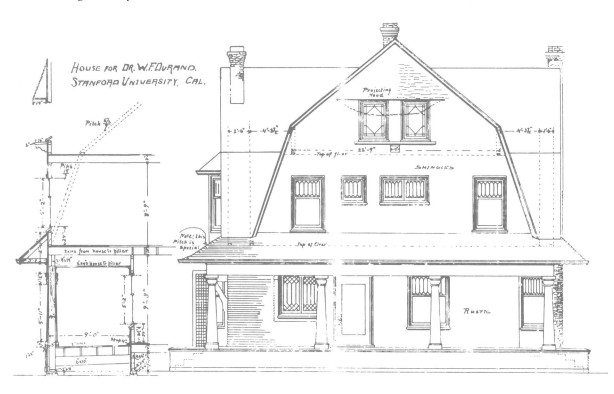

North side

gambrel roofs make several intersections creating a complicated roofline. The exterior finish is rustic on the lower level and shingle on the upper story. The design is unobtrusive and must have seemed so even when the setting was barren except for a single massive oak. Unfortunately shrubbery now hides much of the house and conceals the distant bay view.

Clark used windows in an interesting way throughout the house. Some are bay windows; others cut across corners. Simple geometric patterns in lead are used in many windows. One at the stair landing also uses delicate color to produce a stylized water lily design. This design is repeated in carvings in the living room, in the hall, and on the stair banister and the newel post.

In the dining room a grape motif is used. All the hand carving in the house was done by Professor Clark. The woodwork is unfinished redwood, and large panels of burl redwood are featured above the fireplace mantel and as the back of a handsome hall bench. The balustrade of the staircase is an exception, being made of quarter-sawn Peruvian mahogany. The floors are of Eastern oak, rather than the pine found in most early campus homes.

The Durands added another innovation as well: a circulating-hot-air coal furnace to supplement their five fireplaces. The living room fireplace is surrounded by large tiles of rough texture and a warm brown color. The mantel is flanked by finely carved free-standing columns.

Lou Henry Hoover House

LOU HENRY and Herbert Hoover met while they were students at Stanford University in 1894-95, and were married in 1899. Trained as a mining engineer and strikingly successful in international mining and business ventures, Hoover spent little time in California, but he and his wife always considered Stanford their home.

During World War I, while the Hoovers were living in London, they received permission to build a house on the crest of San Juan Hill. Displeased with the sketches offered by the architect Louis C. Mullgardt, they consulted their friend Professor A. B. Clark. He agreed to serve as an adviser to his son Birge Clark, who had a degree in architecture from Columbia, and Charles Davis, a talented draftsman who had made the drawings for Filoli (p. 110). As the younger Clark recalls, their job was to make structural sense of Mrs. Hoover's far from conventional ideas, and the collaboration worked out well.

According to Hoover's *Memoirs*, his wife's ideas for the house expressed "her own blend of fine living and the new spirit of native western architecture." Whatever the source of her inspiration, the house is unique. Roofs were constructed as usable terraces and connected to one another by outside stairways, thus expanding the area available for entertaining large groups. (Though an outdoor fireplace on one of the roof terraces was built specifically for her sons, they

Lou Henry Hoover House, 1920

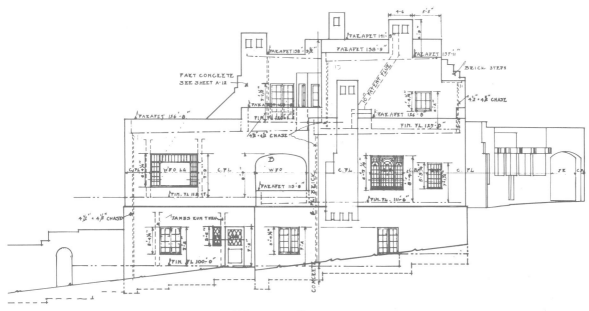

WEST ELEVATION

Outdoor fireplace

preferred campfires on a vacant lot.) Mrs. Hoover wanted the house to conform to the shape of the hill as much as possible to conceal its size. Mr. Hoover's concern with fire dictated the concrete, brick, and hollow tile construction, which was covered with an off-white stucco.

Although leaded glass in geometric and Art Nouveau patterns was used in most windows, Mr. Hoover insisted on plate glass windows in his study. In 1920 Santa Ynez Street went straight up the hill, and friends coming to call used the garden door near the street. After Hoover became President of the United States in 1929, the Secret Service had the road closed along that side of the house, causing visitors to use the main entrance.

For the interior Mrs. Hoover chose a more conventional style, English Tudor, but she was not constrained by it. The entry hall is an octagonal oak-paneled room. Some of the finest workmanship in the house is in the stair hall. After taking measurements, an Oakland craftsman built in his shop the intricate spiral staircase, each detail of which is slightly different from the

Lou Henry Hoover House, 1975

others. Oak paneling was used in all the main rooms, and natural leaf designs created by Professor Clark were carved on newel posts and corbels. The ceiling was coved for indirect lighting in both the living room and the dining room because the Hoovers did not like hanging light fixtures. The dining room was raised two steps so that it might also serve as a stage for amateur theatricals, one of Mrs. Hoover's hobbies. Panels in the dining room conceal cabinets designed for Mrs. Hoover's pewter collection.

Mrs. Hoover wanted fireplaces in every room. In the study an elaborate Tudor-style mantel of oak paneling frames the fireplace. Many of the other mantels are made of Indiana limestone. The living room fireplace was unconventionally placed in an outside corner when Mrs. Hoover proved reluctant to give up either a gallery for displaying her collection of Belgian art objects or any of the French doors onto the terrace. As it turned out, the collection was never brought to the house, and the gallery is now used as a service corridor.

The Hoovers moved into their new home in June 1920 before it was completely finished. But they had only a few months to enjoy the house, because in 1921 Hoover was appointed Secretary

Roof terraces

of Commerce. From then on his public life required him to spend more and more of his time in Washington.

Mr. and Mrs. Hoover returned to their Stanford home as often as possible in the next few years but usually for short visits only. In November 1928 they came home to vote and to hear the election results among their Stanford friends and neighbors. When the outcome was clear, Hoover stepped out onto the terrace to greet the assembled well-wishers and to be serenaded by Stanford students and the visiting John Philip Sousa Band.

Not surprisingly, the unusual house on the hill above Stanford became known as the President's House and carried that name until Mrs. Hoover's death in 1944. At that time Hoover renamed it the Lou Henry Hoover House and donated it to Stanford as a residence for the university's presidents.

Chapter Five

The End of an Era
1900's-1920's

The turn of a century, be it fourteenth, eighteenth, or twentieth, is often used as a watershed in the Western world: after the turn of the century people stopped doing this, or started doing that. But for those who live along that peculiar fracture called the San Andreas Fault, another date—1906—is more commonly used. It was this way before the earthquake, that way after the earthquake. Everyone knows which quake was *the* quake.

In a very obvious way the earthquake changed life on the San Francisco Peninsula by causing its slowly increasing population to become a rapidly increasing population. Train stations became villages and villages turned into towns. Suddenly the peninsula was no longer the preserve of the very wealthy or, on the coastside, a series of picturesque villages with excellent hunting and fishing in between. Aunt May lived down the peninsula and Uncle Harry had a butcher shop in Menlo Park.

The wealthy continued to build homes in the

Gardens at Filoli

Water gardens at Green Gables

foothills, some of them very grand indeed, but there was a subtle difference, or perhaps the difference was subtlety. The foyer of a new mansion was less likely to have opera boxes with silver-plated railings, and game rooms were less likely to be equipped with mother-of-pearl-inlaid pool cues. Filoli was the last of the great mansions, and in style and furnishing it was closer to the cool elegance of an English country house than to the Mississippi riverboat tradition of William C. Ralston. More and more often, however, the wealthy were building houses like Atalaya—spacious family homes in quiet good taste.

San Francisco's rich financiers did not create huge estates from altruistic conservation-oriented motives, but in many cases that has been the effect of their presence on the peninsula. Large tracts of land are available now to be preserved as open space or public parks that might otherwise have been covered with row after row of houses. And in many cases the buildings themselves have changed with the times and been made available for public use. The Payne-Douglass House is now part of the Menlo College campus. Filoli has been given to the National Trust for Historic Preservation. And Atalaya has been promised to Stanford University.

Many of the San Francisco Peninsula's finest buildings did not survive to be adapted for other uses. For them the earthquake truly was the crucial date. Unlike the buildings in this book, far too few of them were carefully preserved in photographs and drawings.

94

La Questa Wine Cellar

AT ONE TIME the San Francisco Peninsula was dotted with small wineries. In 1890, for instance, there were nearly 800 acres of commercial vineyards in the Woodside-Portola Valley area alone. But the peninsula never developed a major wine industry despite its early beginnings, in part because many vineyards were destroyed in the 1880's and 1890's by *Phylloxera vitifoliae*, and many others were torn out after the ratification of the Eighteenth Amendment in 1919.

La Questa was a moderate-sized winery owned by Emmet Hawkins Rixford, a San Francisco attorney. Rixford bought 40 acres on a south slope in the Woodside foothills in 1883 and over the years planted some 17 acres in grapes. Rixford became an authority on his hobby, and even wrote a book for vintners.

Rixford's hobby had become a business by the time his two sons were grown. The elder son, Allen, took over the management of the ranch and winery, and his brother Halsey and their father continued to be actively involved. They grafted vines imported from France on native Phylloxera-resistant root stock. In the 1890's they built a wooden structure to house their wine press and bottling equipment. In 1902 Charles Rosa, a Swiss stonemason, built a wine cellar with the fieldstones the Rixfords had been collecting as they cultivated the vineyards. To provide the cool temperature necessary for storing wine, the cellar was built into the north slope of a hill. Following the earthquake Rosa returned to replace the walls that had crumbled. He apparently finished the job in 1909, for that is the date carved in the arch over the door.

Most peninsula vineyard owners sold their grapes in bulk to larger wineries, but the Rixfords bottled and sold their wine under their own label. They concentrated on cabernet sauvignon, and won international awards for it in 1905 and again in 1915. The Rixfords kept their vineyard going during Prohibition by selling grapes to Italians who made wine for their own use. Financially they found it was more profitable to sell the grapes than the wine, but even so the winery reopened as soon as Prohibition was repealed. La Questa was closed permanently in 1945, and the property was subdivided.

In 1949 Volney O. Chase, a retired engineer and architect, bought the lot with the old wine cellar on it. By then it was a 35′ x 60′ shell, but the walls were a firm 18 inches thick. Chase salvaged the 33-foot-long 3″ x 14″ fir planks used to frame the old wine-press shed, and set about building a frame house within the walls of the original stone cellar. By use of an internal frame, proper support for a second floor could be built without putting weight on the old walls. Additional windows and doors in the old walls were braced with angle irons. To prevent damage from moisture seeping through the old lime mortar, a thick bed of gravel was spread on the original floor before a floating concrete slab was poured.

The big arched entry into the cellar now frames French doors opening into the living room. The second story of the house extends only partway, leaving the living room dramatically open to the full height of the original building.

Church of St. Matthew

IN 1865, when Mr. and Mrs. George H. Howard donated land and initiated construction of the original Episcopal Church of St. Matthew, San Mateo hardly existed. Probably no more than 150 people lived in the surrounding area, but there was a new railroad station, a school, and a blacksmith shop. There were also several large estates in the neighborhood and twelve to fifteen houses for the people who worked on them. The Howard estate, established in 1850 by William Davis Merry Howard, was the first of the elaborate peninsula estates, and it was on Howard's original land purchase that many of the other people later built.

Howard, a Bostonian who started out as a cabin boy on a hide drogher, had accumulated a large fortune by the time he was thirty. At that age he bought a rancho and retired from business in order to become a cattleman. He died at the age of thirty-nine, and his widow married his brother, George H. Howard. It was to William Davis Merry Howard that the new church was dedicated.

The stone church consecrated in May 1865 was Gothic in style and was soon covered with ivy. In the earthquake the building was so badly damaged that it had to be razed. Services con-

By 1950 the congregation of the parish had far exceeded the building's capacity, but the parishioners were unwilling to consider extensions that would endanger the perfection of their church's design. In 1956 Milton T. Pflueger came up with a novel solution. He literally cut the church in half and inched the font end of the nave a full 30 feet to the south. The project was so beautifully engineered that not a single window was broken nor was the plaster cracked. The new section inserted in the space increased the seating to accommodate an additional 160 people. The old English firm of Heaton, Butler and Bayne that had made the original stained-glass windows had gone out of business, so the new windows were created by Henry Lee Willett of Philadelphia.

tinued in the less seriously damaged parish house, while the determined Reverend Neptune Blood William Galwey encouraged his parishioners to begin rebuilding at once.

The architect Willis J. Polk, a member of the parish, was commissioned to design the new church in a style recalling their old village Gothic church. He translated this general requirement into a large, handsome structure. To avoid a repetition of the disaster of 1906, he used a modern steel frame with reinforced concrete and faced it with gray Colusa sandstone laid in a random pattern. The roof forms are both massive and high. The intricate design of the stained-glass window in the font end of the nave combines within a substantial lancet a series of slender ogee and lancet arches topped by a trefoil. The new church was consecrated in May 1910.

Payne-Douglass House

MARY O'BRIEN PAYNE, niece and an heir of William O'Brien of Comstock Lode fame, and her husband Theodore F. Payne, a hardware manufacturer, like many San Franciscans had a summer home on the peninsula. William F. Curlett had designed their Sutter Street home in San Francisco, and they turned to him again to design a new home in Menlo Park. Although it was commissioned in 1906, construction did not begin until the year 1909, probably because of Mr. Payne's death. The house was finished in 1913.

The house Curlett designed was one of the first domestic structures to use reinforced concrete, a technique employed in public structures for a number of years. Intricate design elements had to be cast and then incorporated into the poured walls. Precisely how it was done is not known, but the superb quality of the work suggests a good deal of experience. The interior face of the concrete was furred with wood studs and room partitions were also wood, but everything else, including floor and roof slabs, was reinforced concrete. Much of the lumber used to build forms for the Payne house was reused in the construction of more modest homes in Menlo Park. The final exterior finish was a ⅛-inch coat of sand plaster.

The style of the house was both popular at the time and compatible with the steel and concrete construction. Although it was classified by one architect as "vaguely French Baroque" and by another as French Renaissance, the most reliable statement concludes that it "bears strong 19th Century Italian and French influence." The brief projections of the façade suggest truncated wings, and the slight indentation of the second

Porte cochère

Great Hall

story at the cornice line implies, but does not create, a French mansard. The main entry is through a massive columned porte cochere, with marble stairs leading to a bronze and plate glass door embellished with delicate iron grillwork.

The room count for Mrs. Payne's mansion varies from 52 to 56. The style is one of unrelieved elegance, and nearly all the rooms seem massive and cold. The major rooms have oak parquet floors, some with intricate designs. The windows in the great hall are shaded by sliding screens ornamented with graceful grillwork similar to the wrought-iron balustrade on the central staircase. Ceiling ornamentation is elaborate, picked out in some rooms with gold leaf and color. Carved marble mantels are used throughout the house. The main rooms of the first two floors are paneled in oak.

Leon Forrest Douglass, who bought the Payne house in 1921, was a well-known and prolific inventor of electronic, telephonic, phonographic, and photographic devices. In 1886 he patented the first pay telephone, and in 1894 he perfected the spring motor, an invention that led him, in

partnership with Eldridge Johnson, to form the Victor Talking Machine Company, later known as R.C.A. Victor. The Victrola name was derived from the name of Douglass's wife, Victoria Adams.

Douglass retired from R.C.A. the year after he bought the Payne house, but his experiments continued. The new estate became his workshop. The basement was filled with heavy machinery, and on the mezzanine he installed a moving picture sound laboratory. The only structural change the Douglasses made in the house was to enclose a porch on the east side. In 1935 they built a modest but comfortable bungalow on a corner of the estate, where they lived until his death in 1940 and hers in 1943.

During World War II the mansion was occupied by convalescent soldiers from nearby Dibble Hospital. After the war the house and land were sold to Menlo School and College, which subdivided some of the property and retained the house to use as administrative offices, with faculty housing located on the upper floors. The beautifully paneled library is now the president's office.

Portola (Valley) School

In 1894 Andrew Smith Hallidie, inventor of the cable car, and his wife donated land for a school near the entrance to their estate. A new one-room schoolhouse, complete with bell tower, was built and served the community's needs well into the next century. The census of 1910, however, revealed that, even though the school was already crowded with 53 students, there were actually 76 children who were eligible to attend. This surge of population reflected the new popularity of the Portola Valley area among wealthy San Franciscans. Shunning the earlier summer communities along the railroads, they were now building their mansions among the trees and foothills of Portola Valley, and in the process creating jobs and the need for a larger school.

LeBaron R. Olive, a local architect, was selected by the Board of Trustees in 1909 to make the drawings for the new school and to superintend

Northeast elevation

its construction. Olive drew up plans in Mission Revival, a style in which many California school buildings had been built. Olive, however, interpreted the style in wood rather than stucco. In the heart of a redwood forest, wood construction was much less expensive, and the effect was distinctive.

The characteristic *espadaña* gables with segmented arches, or scallops, are in this interpretation faced with 1″ x 4″ redwood shiplap. Each side gable has a bull's-eye louver, and in the center gable there is a Palladian motif. The recessed porch is accented with two Tuscan columns framing the double-doored entrance, above which is an elegant semicircular fanlight. Simpler fanlights adorn the tops of the two side windows. The columns, cornices, and trim are all of redwood. The exterior walls are sheathed with cedar shingles and 1″ x 8″ channel redwood.

The interior of the little school was finished in pine and left unpainted. A platform at the far end of the room, near the coal stove, held the teacher's desk. Banks of windows on each side of the room provided all the lighting that was to be had.

In later years electricity was added and a shed-roofed addition was put on the back to house a furnace. Cedar shingles on the roof gave way to composition, but the bronze hardware throughout the building has not been changed. Until mid-century, when a city-bred member of the school board decided that all country schools were red, the Portola School was painted white. Population pressure in the 1950's demanded that the one large room be partitioned into two, and for safety one of the windows on each side was made into a door, but no other major alterations have occurred since the building's original construction.

Our Lady of the Wayside

A NUMBER of the summer residents building in Portola Valley around the turn of the century were Catholics, and their nearest church was the friendly but rather plain reconditioned dance hall on the corner of Thomas J. Kelly's land. When the church hierarchy became aware of the change in their flock, they assigned a new priest, Father George L. Lacombe, to ride over from Menlo Park and Atherton each Sunday to say Mass. The choice of priest was excellent, for Lacombe was a sophisticated, well-educated young man who enjoyed people of all classes and religions. His friendship with members of an exclusive men's club, The Family, located near the church was instrumental in the construction of a new build-ing. As Lacombe reported it, the club invited him to lunch one Sunday in June 1911, and before the day was over they were enthusiastically planning

a new church. The architect was decided by a roll of dice, the honor going to James R. Miller, who assigned the project to his young employee, Timothy L. Pflueger. Pflueger later created such modern art deco buildings as the Oakland

Our Lady of the Wayside, 1913

Paramount Theater and San Francisco's innovative Union Square parking garage.

Pflueger used the belfry façade of Mission Dolores in San Francisco as his model and produced a lovely wedding of features from Mission Revival and Georgian. The wide doorway, with its broken pediment, modified Tuscan columns, and entablature, is Georgian. The segmented fanlight over the recessed main door is repeated over each window along the buttressed sides of the building. The reinforced-concrete building was covered with stucco to simulate adobe. It was dedicated in 1912.

The Family gave benefits and contributed much to the building's construction, but local parishioners gave comparable amounts in various ways. For example, one family housed the construction superintendent and others excavated and hauled the gravel donated by yet another family. Most of the building supplies were donated, and all of the furnishings were gifts. The building is truly a monument to the cooperation of many people from a wide variety of backgrounds and religions.

Our Lady of the Wayside, 1975

Green Gables

GREEN GABLES is one of the few homes in northern California designed by the famous southern California architects Charles Sumner Greene and Henry Mather Greene. It was built in Woodside in 1911 to serve as a summer residence for the Mortimer Fleishhackers and is still used in that capacity by the Fleishhacker family.

The Fleishhacker commission was a unique opportunity for the Greenes, since the house was to be designed on a large scale and in climatic conditions quite unlike those they were accustomed to in southern California. The Fleishhackers wanted an English-style house with a simulated thatch roof, and Charles Greene, who had recently been in England, was eager to express some of the things he had learned there. The size and natural beauty of the estate, and the opportunity to design the grounds as well as the house, presented a stimulating challenge to the Greenes' creative minds. Charles Greene spent many hours sitting on the knoll in the Woodside foothills, contemplating the site and its possibilities. The result was a near perfect harmony between the house, the landscaping, and the distant mountains.

The house is an excellent interpretation of turn-of-the-century English country architecture, softening a sophisticated elegance with graciousness and avoiding ostentation by careful attention to scale and proportion. The basic shape is an ell, but variations in the roofline make it seem more complicated. The front angle wraps around

Exposed beams and heavy timbers   *Water gardens, looking toward the house*

Shingled roof showing thatched appearance

a large courtyard. On the back the main wing looks out onto the terrace and a carefully focused view.

To achieve the thatch appearance on the roof, redwood shakes were laid in an irregular pattern. The roll edge was made by steaming and shaping each shingle individually. The use of exposed beams under the eaves and the heavy timbered porches were typical of the Greenes' designs. The use of Gunite (concrete stucco applied under pressure) to cover the frame structure was a technique chosen by Henry Greene for its durability and fire-resistant qualities.

Mrs. Fleishhacker had firm ideas on the interior details of her house, preferring painted walls to the Greenes' usual natural wood. As a result, the rooms are more severe than other Greene interiors, but seem larger, more open, and full of natural light. Such characteristic Greene touches as the wood band around rooms at doortop height and the black oriental trim around panels in the hall are retained, and wood detailing in the gallery and stairwell is present but painted. Elsie de Wolf, an Eastern interior decorator,

Water gardens, from the reflecting pool terrace

designed the interiors, and many of the rooms still have her original furnishings, such as the soft green enameled table and chairs in the dining room.

The terrace and the fenestration of the back of the house were designed around an enormous old valley oak whose loss in 1950 changed the character of the area. The terrace is surfaced with bricks set in sand, using an irregular, informal pattern. Two long gravel paths lead from the terrace across a wide lawn to a lily pond oriented to reflect the full width of the house. Every wall, urn, and balustrade was designed and placed by Charles Greene to provide a continuity between house, garden, and distant mountains.

The Greenes' relationship with Green Gables did not terminate when the house was completed in 1912. In 1916 a free-form swimming pool was built out of sight of the house and reached by a grand brick stairway off the entry courtyard. In 1917 a second floor was added to the servants' wing. In 1924 the garden room was enclosed by Charles Greene, and it expresses fully his artistry. Although smaller than most other rooms in the house, it is the only room paneled in natural

Card Room

wood. The pattern used in the plaster ceiling and tiles is repeated in the carving of the furniture, also designed by Charles Greene. Carvings on cabinets and friezes are thematically integrated depictions of four continents.

In 1927 Charles Greene created the water gardens, which demonstrate his sensitivity to stone as well as wood. Out of sight of the house, the gardens are reached by sloping paths and stairs. The 300′ x 60′ pool ends with open arches, suggesting an old Roman aqueduct, and is constructed of fitted flat stones simulating Roman tiles. Below the balustrade and the stair-paths there is a comparable arched grotto. The overall effect is of old-world beauty fitting harmoniously into the natural California setting.

No one is quite sure of the origin of the name Green Gables, but Mr. Fleishhacker had a weakness for puns. Green Gables may be his sly tribute to the architects who created his beautiful home.

Villa Rose

BUILT IN 1912 in a spectacular setting on the side of a steep canyon in Hillsborough, Villa Rose has been unaffected by the usual incursions of highways and housing developments. Joseph Donahoe Grant, born in San Francisco in 1858, was a prominent civic and business leader on the West Coast. After the Grants' Italian-style villa near the Burlingame Country Club was destroyed by fire, they asked a friend, Lewis Hobart, the architect for San Francisco's Grace Cathedral, to design and landscape another house on the property.

In orienting the house, Hobart made excellent use of the sloping site. A terrace along one side drops to a lawn from which inviting paths wander among masses of azaleas and rhododendrons under the oaks. Appreciative of the natural beauty of their surroundings, the Grants used much care in the construction of a driveway, building terraces where necessary to keep the canyon from eroding. In the canyons they planted redwoods.

The house Hobart designed is modest in its proportions, but is considered an unusually pure rendering of Italian Renaissance in the Florentine tradition. The simple rectangular lines of the style adapt well to the reinforced-concrete construction. The name Villa Rose comes from the soft rose tint added to the concrete.

The formal main entry to the house is from a walled courtyard. A portico supported by modified Tuscan columns with the appropriate classical detailing of frieze, cornice, and dentil course covers the door. The windows on either side of the portico have decorated keystones in their arches and an Italian Renaissance design

Christopher Wren Room

in the lunettes, a design repeated elsewhere. The upstairs windows are all ornamented by fine wrought-iron balustrades. The same balustrade appears on a balcony supported by modified Tuscan columns on the south end of the house.

The Grants used Villa Rose almost exclusively as a country retreat, limiting their entertaining there to close friends. When they were traveling, their children lived there rather than in the city.

In 1936 Villa Rose was sold to Mr. and Mrs. Charles R. Blyth, who changed the name to Strawberry Hill and used the estate as a year-round residence. Blyth, a leading investment banker, and his wife did much entertaining at Strawberry Hill. The grounds were changed very little, but the interior was extensively renovated.

The entry hall is a large, square early-English-style room, paneled in natural oak with carved molding and panel borders. The paneling is carried into the stairway hall, as is the black-and-white marble floor. The newel post and balustrade of the stairway are hand-carved. A Louis XIII brass candelabrum lights the entry hall, and a crystal chandelier lights the stairway hall. The natural oak paneling of both halls is repeated in the library. On the walls of the dining room there are five large murals by D. Dalens,

dated 1746. The Blyths replaced the downstairs floors with 400-year-old English parquet.

The most significant change the Blyths made in the house was in the "garden room" on the south end. Under the supervision of their designer, Francis Lenygon of New York, a room designed by Christopher Wren about 1695 was removed from Blith Hall in Yorkshire and installed in Strawberry Hill. The room has oak paneling with acanthus leaf designs carved in the molding, exquisite double doors, and a massive black marble mantel. The room has two Waterford crystal chandeliers.

For their drawing room, a room the Blyths referred to as the Chinese Room, hand-painted eighteenth-century chinoiserie wallpaper was removed from Harlaxton Manor in Grantham (England). Each of the large birds in the paper is a unique design. The room also has been given an eighteenth-century carved marble mantel.

Filoli

FILOLI, the lovely Georgian Revival brick house set among ancient oaks near Woodside, was designed by Willis J. Polk for William Bowers Bourn II and his wife. Bourn, one of San Francisco's most successful entrepreneurs, derived the name of his country estate from the three words that epitomized his philosophy: fight, love, live. Filoli was the third house Polk designed for the Bourns, and it is considered his finest domestic work in the twentieth century. The plans were signed in 1915, and the Bourns occupied the house two years later.

Filoli is U-shaped, contains 18,000 square feet in its two stories, and is divided into approximately 40 rooms. The red tile roof is hipped and has three dormer windows in the front and back sides of the central section. Beneath the eaves are classical white carved stone modillions or cornice blocks. The main entrance to the house is

covered by a portico supported by Doric columns
and topped by a stone balustrade. All of the
French windows on the ground floor are arched.
Each second-floor window has a wrought-iron
balcony.

Filoli's rooms are large; ceilings on the main
floor are twenty feet high. The entrance hall has
a white marble floor, but most of the other down-

stairs rooms are laid with parquet. Wide halls
cross the house on both floors. The lower hallway
is segmented by a series of pilastered arches.

The ballroom fills the $1\frac{1}{2}$-story right wing. Its
crystal chandeliers once hung in the room
where the Treaty of Versailles was signed. The
Ernest Peixotto murals were commissioned by the
Bourns in 1925. They depict scenes from the

Ballroom

Lakes of Killarney, the Irish estate the Bourns purchased for their daughter after her marriage in 1910 and later gave to the government for a national park. The enormous fireplace is of green marble decorated with ormolu.

Other rooms on the main floor include a library and a dining room paneled in straight-grain walnut. The drawing room was originally furnished with French furniture to complement the Bourns' collection of French prints. The left wing of the building contains kitchens, pantries, the silver safe, and living quarters for the servants.

Construction of the various outbuildings was delayed until after World War I, and the commission for them was given to another architect. At the time Filoli was built, Polk's fondness for alcohol prompted Bourn to pay his commission in the form of a trust fund for Mrs. Polk. Polk was furious and the two old friends ceased speaking to each other. Arthur Brown, Jr. designed the detached service unit in 1918, and it harmonizes well with the mansion. On it a graceful clock tower topped by a crowing-rooster weather vane can be seen from the sunken garden.

From the outset Bourn planned to keep his 700 acres as a game preserve. This created a slight complication for the design of the sixteen acres of formal gardens, since deer draw no distinction between manzanita and rose bushes. Each garden was enclosed, given its own theme, and oriented for the best view of the distant lake or mountains.

The landscape architect was Bruce Porter. His design was completed in 1920 and has been altered very little since.

Bourn suffered a paralytic stroke in 1922 and spent the rest of his life at Filoli. Both he and his wife died in 1936. The estate, including the furnishings, books, and artwork, was sold to the William P. Roths in 1937, who maintained it almost exactly as it had been created. In 1975 they auctioned off most of the furnishings, and gave the house and gardens to the National Trust for Historic Preservation.

Dining Room

Y.W.C.A. Hostess House

Hostess House, 1975

DURING World War I the War Department asked the Young Women's Christian Association to build, equip, and staff a number of Hostess Houses. These structures were to be located in forty Army training camps to provide dignified meeting places for women and their military husbands, friends, or relatives. Camp Fremont, the peninsula's contribution to the war effort, was located in Menlo Park, and its Hostess House was built on Santa Cruz Avenue where the Presbyterian Church stands today.

Julia Morgan, who was just beginning to receive national acclaim as an architect, had designed a number of Y.W.C.A. buildings, including the handsome conference facilities at Asilomar in Pacific Grove, California. Born and raised in the Bay Area, she was in 1894 the first woman to earn a B.S. degree in civil engineering at the University of California. In 1902 she was the first woman to earn a *diplôme* from the Ecole des Beaux Arts in Paris. Two years later she opened an architectural office in San Francisco.

Morgan regarded architecture as the fine art of mechanics, and in responding to the rock-bottom budget allowed for the Hostess House at Camp Fremont, she expressed this fully. Using ordinary materials in an economical way, she attained a grace not common to Army buildings. The one-story, H-shaped frame building was sheathed in board and batten. The exposed wooden trusses under the roof were highlighted

from six long, low dormer windows. At both ends of the central room deep balconies overhung enormous, brick fireplaces. Numerous window-doors opened invitingly onto wide verandas.

Camp Fremont had a short life, and after the war its buildings were sold and moved or dismantled. The Hostess House had functioned so well as a public meeting place that a group of Palo Altans thought its role should be continued in the larger community. The Y.W.C.A. agreed to donate the building to the City of Palo Alto, and Julia Morgan, who kept rigid control over buildings she designed, met with the city's committee and approved the oak-studded site they had leased from Stanford University. The

East elevation

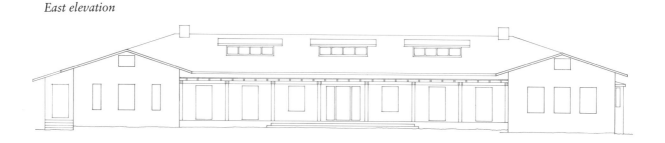

Interior, 1920

building was raised four feet to allow for the installation of a heating system.

By leasing the land and providing funds for the maintenance of the building as well as the minimum salaries for a director and an athletics director, Palo Alto became the first city to give tangible support to the new concept of community centers. Community House, as the building was named, became a living room for the whole town. It was open daily from 9:00 A.M. to 10:30 P.M., with certain hours set aside for lectures and concerts. It ran an active employment bureau and a child-care center. The nucleus of the city's recreation and parks program took form in Community House, and its night-school classes became so popular that they had to be taken over by the public schools. In 1930, when a larger community center building was donated to the city, coals from the fireplaces at Community House were carried to the new center to symbolize the hope that the original spirit of Community House would continue in the new buildings.

The Veterans' Council now leases the building for a nominal fee. They have either covered or removed the evidence of the architect's inspiration: her buildings were known for their clean, well-defined lines. But no major structural changes have been made, and the integrity of Julia Morgan's original design could be restored.

Atalaya

J. HENRY MEYER was a leading San Francisco
financier and a major influence in California's
development. He and his wife lived for a time in
Berkeley, but were advised that the sunnier
weather of the peninsula would be better for their
son's bronchial condition. In 1900 they bought
Eugene Avy's Menlo Park summer home, and
after some additions and renovations made it their
year-round home. The name for the house was
suggested by a Spanish visitor who thought the
Queen Anne turret on the house and its setting
on a rocky bluff above the flatland gave it the
appearance of an *atalaya*, or watchtower.

In 1918 the Avy house burned. Meyer, whose
wife had died the year before, commissioned his
friend Arthur Brown, Jr. to design a new house.
At the time Brown was receiving much praise
for the recently completed San Francisco City
Hall and his designs for other civic buildings.
Both Brown and Meyer had strong preferences
for French styles of architecture. Meyer had been
educated in Geneva, and Brown had studied at
the Ecole des Beaux Arts. The house Brown
designed is in the Second Renaissance Revival
or French Mediterranean style.

Meyer and his family wanted a dignified but
livable house, not a grand showplace. Although
modest if compared with such mansions as
Filoli, the house is generously proportioned. It
is sheathed with a fine cream-colored stucco, and
its red-tiled hip roof is edged by a concrete

View from the back lawn

balustrade of the same design as the balustrades that line the terrace. The upstairs windows all have intricately designed wrought-iron balconies.

The relaxed openness that Meyer desired is expressed in the interior floor plan by the easy circulation through the rooms of the lower floor. Each room opens into the one next to it as well as onto a connecting hall. There is also direct access from the main floor rooms to the terrace across the rear of the house. The major furnishings were imported from France. Some of them, such as the hand-carved dining room furniture, were designed for Meyer in Paris. The antique statues on each side of the front entry were also brought from France. They are replicas of statues at the Palace of Versailles.

Meyer died shortly after his new home was completed, but his children have continued to live in the house. In 1940, a young botanist, Ernest Matthews, brought experience gained in Kew Gardens and several English estates to Atalaya. Since then he has supervised the maintenance of the original landscaping and added many beautiful gardens to it. The seven-acre Atalaya grounds now rival the house in significance.

It was announced by the family in 1970 that Atalaya has been bequeathed to Stanford University with an endowment for its maintenance. It is to be "preserved and devoted to uses beneficial to the University." Atalaya is only one of many generous gifts made by the Meyers to Stanford University.

Bibliography

This Bibliography consists of publications that I found especially useful in doing research for this book. Other useful publications on the history of San Mateo and Santa Clara counties and their localities are listed in Margaret Miller Rocq for the California Library Association, *California Local History: A Bibliography* (Stanford: 1970) and its 1976 *Supplement*.

Alexander, Philip W., and Charles P. Hamm. *History of San Mateo County*. Burlingame: Burlingame Publishing Co., 1916.

Atherton, Gertrude. *Adventures of a Novelist*. New York: Liveright, 1932.

——— *California: An Intimate History*. New York: Harpers, 1914.

Bancroft, Hubert Howe. *History of California*. 7 vols. San Francisco: History Co., 1884-90.

Barnes, Mary Sheldon. "History Hunting in Spanish Town," *Stanford Sequoia*, May 11, 1892.

Berner, Bertha. *Mrs. Leland Stanford*. Stanford: Stanford University Press, 1934.

Bowers, Nathan A. "Life Begins at Sixty-Five—" (guest editorial), *Aeronautical Engineering Review*, June 1951.

Cady, Theron G. *Tales of the San Francisco Peninsula*. San Carlos: C-T Publishers, 1948.

Century 67, Redwood City Historical Trail. Pamphlet published by the City of Redwood City, 1967.

Cipriani, Count. *California and Overland Journals, 1849-1862*. Ernest Falbo, ed. Portland, Ore.: Champoeg Press, 1962.

Clark, Birge M. *Memoirs about Mr. and Mrs. Herbert Hoover with Particular Emphasis on the Planning and Building of Their Home on San Juan Hill*. Privately printed, Palo Alto, 1969.

Clark, George T. *Leland Stanford*. Stanford: Stanford University Press, 1931.

Cloud, Roy W. *History of San Mateo County*. 2 vols. Chicago: S. J. Clarke, 1928.

Davidson, George. *Pacific Coast Pilot*. 4th ed. Washington, D.C.: U.S. Government Printing Office, 1889.

DeFord, Miriam Allen. "Palo Alto's Mysterious Frenchman," *California Historical Society Quarterly*, XXXIII, 1954.

Durand, W. F. *Adventures*. New York: McGraw-Hill, 1953.

Duveneck, Josephine W. "The Community House," *School Arts Magazine*, XX, 5 (Jan. 1921), 253-58.

Elliott, Ellen Coit. *It Happened This Way*. Stanford: Stanford University Press, 1940.

Elliott, Orrin Leslie. *Stanford University: The First Twenty-Five Years*. Stanford: Stanford University Press, 1937.

Evans, Albert S. *A La California: Sketches of Life in the Golden State*. San Francisco: Bancroft, 1873.

Evans, Elliot. *Burlingame, Its Railroad Station, an American Classic*. Pamphlet issued at the dedication of State Historic Landmark No. 846. San Mateo County Historical Association, 1971.

"Filoli," *Country Life*, June 1937, pp. 30-40.

[Frazier, P. Munroe, and William L. Halloway.] *History of San Mateo County, California*. San Francisco: B. F. Alley, 1883.

"A Garden Masterpiece," *House & Garden*, July 1966, p. 90.

Garnett, Porter. *Stately Homes of California*. Boston: Little, Brown, 1915.

Gebhard, David, et al. *A Guide to Architecture in San Francisco and Northern California.* Santa Barbara: Peregrine Smith, 1973.

Grant, Joseph D. *Redwoods and Reminiscences.* San Francisco: Save-the-Redwoods League, 1973.

Guinn, J. M. *History of the State of California and Biographical Record of Coast Counties.* Chicago: Chapman, 1904.

Hayne, F. Bourn. "Biography of William Bowers Bourn II." MS, privately printed (n.d.).

Historical Atlas Map of Santa Clara County. San Francisco: Thompson & West, 1876. Reproduced by Smith & McKay, San Jose, 1971.

Holland, Francis Ross, Jr. *America's Lighthouses.* Brattleboro, Vt.: Stephen Greene Press, 1972.

Hoover, Herbert C. *Memoirs.* 3 vols. New York: Macmillan, 1951-52.

Hoover, Mildred Brooke, Hero Eugene Rensch, and Ethel Grace Rensch. *Historic Spots in California.* 3d ed., revised by William N. Abeloe. Stanford: Stanford University Press, 1966.

"An Image of True Luxuriance," *House & Garden,* May 1965, pp. 155-57.

Irwin, Will. *Herbert Hoover.* New York: Grosset & Dunlap, 1928.

Jordan, David Starr. *The Days of a Man.* 2 vols. Yonkers-on-Hudson, N.Y.: World Book Co., 1922.

Kirker, Harold. *California's Architectural Frontier.* New York: Russell & Russell, 1970.

Koch, Margaret. *Santa Cruz County Parade of the Past.* Fresno: Valley Publishers, 1973.

McCoy, Esther. *Five California Architects.* New York: Praeger, 1975.

Makinson, Randell L. *Lives & Work of Greene and Greene.* Santa Barbara: Peregrine Smith, forthcoming.

Milbank, Robbins. [History] *1864-1958.* Pamphlet published by the Church of St. Matthew, San Mateo, 1958.

Mirrielees, Edith R. *Stanford: The Story of a University.* New York: Putnam, 1959.

Mirrielees, Edith R., ed. *Stanford Mosaic.* Stanford: Stanford University, 1962.

Moore, Alexander. "A Pioneer of '47." MS, Bancroft Library, Berkeley.

Moore & DePue's Illustrated History of San Mateo County. San Francisco: G. T. Brown & Co., 1878. Reproduced by G. Richards, San Francisco, 1974.

Nelson, Janet, and Fran Meyer. *Ranchos "Victorian."* Pamphlet, Hillsborough Schools, 1966.

Olmsted, Roger, and T. H. Watkins. *Here Today.* San Francisco: Chronicle Books, 1968.

"Radcliffe Hall," *California Commerce* (San Francisco), vol. I, no. 4 (March 1897), 14-15.

Regnery, Mrs. David C. (Dorothy F.) *Buelna's Indestructible Roadhouse.* San Mateo: San Mateo County Historical Association, 1969.

Robinson, Edgar Eugene, and Paul Carroll Edwards. *The Memoirs of Ray Lyman Wilbur.* Stanford: Stanford University Press, 1960.

Scott, T. B. "Biography of Leland Stanford and History of His Memorial University." MS, Palo Alto Historical Association Archives, 1923.

[Southern Pacific.] *Central California Illustrated.* Los Angeles: California Publishing Co., 1900.

Stanger, Frank M. "The Half Moon Bay Community Methodist Church." MS, San Mateo County Historical Museum Archives, 1949.

———— *History of San Mateo County.* San Mateo: A. H. Cawston, 1938.

———— *Peninsula Community Book.* San Mateo: A. H. Cawston, 1946.

———— *Sawmills in the Redwoods.* San Mateo: San Mateo County Historical Association, 1967.

———— *South from San Francisco.* San Mateo: San Mateo County Historical Association, 1963.

Steele, Catherine, and Wilfred H. Steele. "The Steeles of Point Año Nuevo. Their Ancestry and Kinships." Privately printed, 1971.

Steele, Catherine Baumgarten. "The Steele Brothers," *California Historical Society Quarterly,* XX (Sept. 1941), 259-73.

Turner, Paul V., Marcia E. Vetrocq, and Karen Weitze. *The Founders & the Architects. The Design of Stanford University.* Stanford: Department of Art, Stanford University, 1976.

Tutorow, Norman E. *Leland Stanford: Man of Many Careers.* Menlo Park: Pacific Coast Pub., 1971.

Vischer, Edward. *Vischer's Pictorial of California.* 2 vols. San Francisco, 1870.

Whiffen, Marcus. *American Architecture Since 1780.* Cambridge, Mass.: M.I.T. Press, 1969.

Williams, Henry Lionel, and Attalie K. Williams. *Treasury of Great American Houses.* New York: Putnam, 1970.

Wood, Dallas E., ed. *History of Palo Alto*. Palo Alto: A. H. Cawston, 1939.

Deeds, maps, vital statistics, liens, records of incorporations and court cases, and minutes of meetings of boards of supervisors in the offices of the Clerk and the Recorder of San Francisco, San Mateo, and Santa Clara counties have been searched for important facts. Also used were the minutes and records of councils, planning commissions, and committees of various local communities on the Peninsula. Further information was found in the following libraries and archives:

American Institute of Architects, New York
California, State of:
    Parks & Recreation Department, Historic Preservation Section, Sacramento
    State Library, Sacramento
    State Archives, Sacramento
    University of California, libraries at Berkeley, Davis, Los Angeles, and Santa Cruz, particularly Bancroft Library and Environmental Design Library at Berkeley

California Historical Society, San Francisco
Historic American Buildings Survey, Washington, D.C.
Library of Congress, Washington, D.C.
Maritime Museum, San Francisco
National Archives, San Bruno, California, and Washington, D.C.
National Park Service, Washington, D.C.
Palo Alto Historical Association
San Francisco City Library
Society of California Pioneers, San Francisco
San Mateo County Historical Association
Spanishtown Historical Society, Half Moon Bay
Stanford University
United States Coast Guard, 12th District, San Francisco
Wells Fargo Bank History Room, San Francisco
Wine Institute, San Francisco

Information was also obtained from magazine and newspaper files, interviews, and correspondence with persons familiar with the buildings.

D.F.R.

Index